NICOLAS GUILLEN

GROWTH OF A REVOLUTIONARY CONSCIOUSNESS

J.A.George Irish

CARIBBEAN RESEARCH CENTER
Medgar Evers College
City University of New York

JAGPI PRODUCTIONS
Box 5, Plymouth Montserrat

and

CARIBBEAN RESEARCH CENTER
Medgar Evers College
City University of New York

COVER DESIGN: EION A. SAUNDERS

ISBN: 976-8039-05-1

To the memory of

a dear friend

NICOLÁS GUILLÉN

(July 1902 - July 1989)

and

For my children:

Ayanna,

Ken, Jaja, Jagpi Gershom

as they dream of creativity

and service to humanity.

PREFACE

This book comes as a response to some of the searching questions asked by my students about Revolutionary Cuban Literature and the role of Nicolás Guillén as a mulatto in that Revolutionary situation, and partly in recognition of a wider need for critical commentary by West Indians on Caribbean literature in Spanish.

The book is not an exhaustive study but it attempts to deal with some of the major areas of the poet's work, and to make occasional cross-references to the works of other Caribbean poets like Aimé Césaire, E. Kamau Brathwaite and Derek Walcott.

It is written with the student of African-American literature in mind and therefore assumes a basic familiarity with the major writers in English, French and Spanish in the Caribbean. However it is intended to reach a much wider readership, and for that reason, I have used my own English translations of original Spanish quotes.

CONTENTS

CHAPTER ONE

INTRODUCTION

THE REPUBLICAN MOULD

The Cuban Republic that shaped the character and destiny of Nicolás Guillén came into being in May 1902. Niccolás Guillén himself was born in July, 1902. The significance of this virtual synchronism is not to be overlooked for there is a dramatic correspondence between the growth of the Republican experience and the personal development of Guillén towards his heroic status as Cuba's national poet. It would be difficult to appreciate the real value of his work without relating it to the range of crises and traumas that have checkered Cuba's experience between 1898 and 1959 - the North American presence, the deplorable condition of the Negro, the anxieties of the veterans and liberals over corruption in national politics, the vagaries and hostilities of party politics prior to the Revolution, the sugar saga of the twentieth century, the rise of political activists in the University and their impact on national politics, and the viciousness of dictatorship and political gerrymandering.

SEARCH FOR FREEDOM

The birth of the Republic was a major landmark in the prolonged struggle for liberation by the Cuban people. This is a struggle that began to assume definitive proportions in the October 10, 1868 declaration of independence in Oriente Province which gave rise to a historic popular revolt against Spanish domination, a revolt that claimed an estimated four hundred thousand (400,000) lives among the Cubans and an estimated eighty thousand (80,000) lives among Spanish soldiers. This was followed by another outburst on February 24, 1895 when José Martí, "the apostle of Cuban independence", led his people into the revolutionary explosion that eventually ended abortively in the transfer of power from Spain to the U.S. in the Treaty of Paris on December 10, 1898.

Notwithstanding the political, diplomatic and military sleight of hand of Spanish and U.S. authorities successively, there always was a strong under-current of unrest and anxiety for freedom seething beneath the political surface, particulary among the liberal thinkers and the mass of the people. The suppression of the Ten Years' War of 1868 did little to contain that burning desire for independence. The inhumanities perpetrated by Spanish military authorities in the 1895 revolutionary struugle and the discourtesies of the American successors to power after 1898 did little to dispirit the Cuban people or to dampen their zeal for independence. The names of Antonio Maceo, Máximo Gómez, Juan Gualberto Gómez, Martín Morúa Delgado, Flor Crombet, Périco Pérez and Bartolomé Masó recall that spirit of nationalism which refused to accept Spanish rule, annexation to the U.S. or the Platt-Amendment[1] and demanded full autonomy and universal adult suffrage. The dissatisfaction of the people themselves which became manifest in the very early part of the American occupation - the dock strikes in Havana, Cardenas and Regla in January 1899, followed by strikes of builders and tobacco workers in August, "almost reaching the dimensions of a general strike in September"[2] combined with the call by some sectors of the Press for revolutionary and nationalist insurrection in the hills, to give substance and form to the people's continued pursuit of national liberation.

This is the background against which the Republican era was ushered in with elections of some kind being finally held, and the new Cuban Congress convened, a new Constitution adopted and the Cuban flag hoisted on May 20, 1902. The next fifty-seven years represent the decisive period in Cuba's final struggle for liberation from external powers. It was not until 1959 that Martís disciple, Fidel Castro, and his guerilla forces were able to lead the Cuban people into what has come to be regarded as this hemisphere's first truly popular socialist Revolution.

INHERITED WOUNDS

The attainment of Republican status in 1902 had brought in its wake a chain of inherited wounds. This humiliation of Spain by the U.S. in the short-lived war of 1898, although convenient at the time for the Cuban warriors for independence, remained an unpleasant memory for a people whose deepest sentiments were embedded in a strong Spanish tradition and in an indestructible Spanish cultural connection. The outcry of the Nicaraguan poet, Rubén Darío, against the growing American outrage in his poems, "A Roosevelt" and "Los Cisnes"[3] was a response shared by José Enrique Rodó and other Latin Americans, including Cubans, who felt the anguish of Spanish defeat and the bitterness of American victory through military intervention.

The second major wound had been inflicted by way of the highhanded diplomatic maneuvers of the U.S. during and after the Spanish- American war. According to Scheer and Zeitlin: "During the few months of battle, the U.S. Government treated the Cubans with little respect, and failed even to give them formal recognition as allies. Cubans were not invited to the Spanish surrender of Santiago, and the United States appointed General Leonard Wood military Governor without consulting them. The United States prevented Cuba from being represented at the Paris conference where the treaty which brought the war to an end was discussed and signed on 10th December, 1898".[4]

While Rodó and Darío were protesting from outside, Martí's faithful friend and partner, Juan Gualberto Gómez, continued consistently and persistently to uphold the principles of self-determination and non-intervention from outside powers. His comment on the Platt Amendent, for example illustrates the clear and firm position he took against American imperialism:

> To reserve to the U.S. the faculty of deciding for themselves when independence is menaced and when therefore they ought to intervene to preserve it is equivalent to delivering up the key to our house so that they can enter it at all hours when the desire takes them, day or night...[5]

And experience has proven that his fears were justified. The presence of the Amerians at Guantanamo Bay occupying forty-five (45) square miles of Cuban territory at rental of $2,000.00 a year and without a terminal date being set for the lease, has been a continuous source of embarrassment and irritation for the Cuban Republic. It further became obvious that, "United States interventionist policy was aimed at the creation of political mechanisms that could favour economic penetration".[6] This is what provoked spokesmen like Manuel Sanguily and Salvador Cisneros Betancourt to denounce the U.S. commercial interests and economic domination of Cuba.

The third significant wound bequeathed to Cubans was the overbearing feeling of American superiority over Hispanic peoples which was promulgated by Roosevelt, particulary in his attitude to Cuba, Colombia, and Panama. Hugh Thomas, in a chapter of his book entitled"Cuba Prostrate" points to the "mild yet undeniable racism of Anglo-Saxon Americans (which) was evident not only in speeches of politicians", but in the bureaucratic analysis of "the hard-working census-takers who worked effectively in Cuba in 1899" to prove the inferiority of the black race. Thomas even goes as far as to say that Juan Guslberto Gómez' opposdition to the American presence and his fears over the possibility of annexation were largely due to his concern over the implications of such expressions of racism.[7]

The fourth serious wound, and one that was to affect Guillén deeply, was the actual plight of the Negro whose heritage did not offer any real scope for fulfillment or development. Hugh Thomas makes the following crucial observations on the situation of the black community in Cuba: there were more whites; the number of farms owned by black or mulatto people were five percent of the total and they rented eighteen-and-a-half percent - a total of just under a quarter; no Negro or mulatto owned a farm larger than one hundred and sixty-five acres; most of the very small farms under eight acres were owned and rented by them; these farms were generally small and poor; they had little hold in the cattle area of Camagüey; nine-tenths of the sugar cane was produced by white farmers; tobacco production was similarly white controlled; illiteracy in Cuba embraced about three-fifths of the population; Negroes were ill-established in several key areas - among merchants, government officials, physicians, dentists, policemen, printers, fishermen, sailors and boatmen, saloon keepers, factory workers, teachers, veterinary surgeons, watch-makers, architects, draftsmen, artists, blacksmiths, journalists, clerks, copy-typists, stenographers, telephone and telegraph employees and lawyers; they were however, well established in some professions and crafts as bakers, carpenters, launderers, builders, shoemakers, seamstresses, tailors, domestic servants and musicians.[8]

POLITICAL UNREST

The prevailing socio-economic and political conditions of the first two decades of the Republican era fostered a continuous ferment of dissatisfaction, unrest and repeated uprisings in various sectors of the country. First, it was the Liberal veterans like General Pino Guerra, Eduardo Guzmán, Orestes Ferrara, Colonel Asbert, General Loynaz del Castillo and Evaristo Estenoz who revolted in the 1906 "Guerrita de agosto" in protest against the reelection of Estrada Palma for a second term. This led to the second intervention by the U.S. under the Presidency of Theodore Roosevelt in October 1906. In spite of the U.S. military presence, there were sporadic outbursts in 1906 - 1907 with insurrectionists taking to the hills and carrying on a struggle in the name of Cuban nationalism.

In 1907 there were a number of strikes among cigar workers, stevedores, bus drivers, box makers, plumbers, broom makers, carpenters and railway workers. The best organized of them the "Huelga de la Moneda" among cigar workers lasted for one hundred and forty-five days. Then came the formation of a Negro political party, the Independent Party of Colour led by Evaristo Estenoz, an articulate Negro Liberal who built his campaign on the grievances of Negro veterans who had contributed so significantly to the struggle for independence but who now felt relegated to an under-privileged position in the society.

In the meantime, the Negro population which had been virtually decimated in the Wars of Independence, grew proportionately less as Spanish migrants swarmed into Cuba. In the first decade of the Republican era, almost two hundred thousand (200,000) Spaniards, mainly Galicians and Asturians immigrated to Cuba and swelled the ranks of the whites, and indirectly intensified the Negroes' fears of having to accept a minority and inferior status in the society they had helped to defend and build.

Between 1910 and 1912 the Independent Party of Color was one of the leading pressure groups in the island. Two of its leaders were arrested in 1910 but that did not crush the Negro spirit of protest and revolt. By 1912 an outbreak of demonstrations and strikes developed into a full-scale uprising led by strong Negro leaders such as Evaristo Estenoz and Isidro Santos Carrero. This provided the third opportunity for U.S. intervention when the U.S. Marines were sent in to put an end to the Negro revolts.

At the same time, the veterans were on the war-path once more. General Vicenter Mirel denounced the Government of José Miguel Gómez for tyrannical attempts at muzzling the press and took to the hills in 1912. General Guillermo Acevedo attempted a revolution in Havana province and General Emilio Núñez led the veterans in protest demonstrations that eventually escalated into an open attack by the veterans on Spanish sympathizers and Spanish civil servants who had favored Spain during the Independence War of 1895 - 1898. The matter was only resolved, at least temporarily, in March, 1912. In fact, the veterans went back into action around 1923 - 1924 in an armed revolt against the corruption of Alfredo Zayas' government.

During these years, there was constant anxiety over the extent of corruption in national politics. When in 1908, José Miguel Gómez became President of Cuba with Alfredo Zayas as his Vice-President, it was the result of a concerted effort by the liberals to patch up their internal differences in order to keep Tomás Estrada Palma out of the Presidency. It was a victory for one of Cuba's most popular politicians who had been kept out of the 1905 elections by the sleight of hand that allowed Estrada Palma to be re-elected unopposed on the party ticket of the Moderates (Republican/Conservatives) who had reverted to political violence as a means of harassing and embarrassing the Liberals.

The years 1916 and 1917 were years of grave poltical unrest and social upheaval. Factionalism still plagued the Liberals (Gómez vs Zayas; Zayas vs

Mchado and Mendienta; Zayas vs Hernández), and corruption remained one of the highlights of the Conservative administration. Provoked by alleged electoral fraud in November 1916 when Menocal was reelected, the Liberals staged a seven-month revolt with veterans such as José Miguel Gómez, Zayas (the defeated Presidential candidate) General Machado and Colonel Mendieta in the fore-front. It was not until May, 1917 that Menocal was eventually sworn in for his second term as President, thanks to the fourth intervention and occupation by U.S. marines lasting until 1922.

This liberal revolt which caused the assassination of Guillén's father is one of the historic events that wounded the spirit of the young fifteen-year-old poet most deeply. The folly of party politics of the times and the atrocities of dictatorship and self-interest as he witnessed them even at that early age undoubtedly help to explain his apathy towards and disillusionment with national politics. And yet, they must have helped to mould his sensibility for later years when those very themes came to the surface in the poetry of his adult years.

THE NINETEEN TWENTIES

Then came the economic crisis following the "unnatural sugar prosperity" brought on by World War I. The price of sugar up to July 1914 was 1.93 cents per pound, but the heavy demands for sugar during the war lifted the Cuban price and production to unusual levels. Sales to the U.S. and Britain were rising constantly and the demand for foreign labour increased. Between 1914 and 1918, twenty-seven thousand (27,000) Haitians, twenty-three thousand (23,000) Jamaicans, plus Chinese and West Indian workers were imported. "In 1919 alone, about twenty-four thousand (24,000) Jamaicans arrived along with ten thousand (10,000) Haitians."[9] By 19th May, 1920, the price had reached twenty-two and one-half cents (22 1/2 cents) per pound, largely owing to a meteoric rise following the lifting of wartime controls on prices, in 1920, but by this time, so much sugar was available on the World Market that it did not take long for the price to drop. Between June and December it slid from seventeen and one-half cents to three and three-quarters cents. The slump affected banking arrangements, orders, shipping and storage, particularly for the owners of mills.

The next major development involved University reform prompted by student demonstrations in 1922 against corruption and incompetence in the appointment and performance of academic and administrative staff. This had serious political implications since many of the culprits were merely political henchmen. Progressive professors such as Enrique José Varona and Fernando Ortiz on the one hand and the rector of Havana University, Carlos de la Torre, in their separate ways, pressed for varying levels of university reform, while students, through the newly formed University Students' Federation (FEU) spearheaded by their secretary, Julio Antonio Mella, made heavy demands for reform in the University as well as in national politics. The students' activities were firmly supported by adult protest groups, some literary men like, Rubén Martínez Villena, José Z. Tallet, Jorge Mañach, Juan Marinello, Alberto Lamar Schweyer, and Alejo Carpentier, as well as other distingushed Cubans such as Colonel Mendieta, Manuel Sanguily, Hernández Cartaya and Enrique Varona, during the very tense months of 1923. The end result of all this feverish activity was the rejection of Zayas as a possible Conservative candidate for the 1924 elections.

This paved the way for a swing towards the Liberals whose candidate General Gerardo Machado, defeated ex-President Menocal and became President in 1925. The Machado era which lasted until 1933 has come to be regarded as a reign of terror in Cuban politics. Students, writers, intellectuals, labour leaders, possible political opponents, Spanish anarchists, socialists and communists were rounded up by the scores and persecuted, deported, imprisoned or shot unscrupulously and systematically. His military agents worked effectively in schools, in the civil service, in commerce and industry and in the lottery to ensure that the President's interests were defended and promoted. For Guillén, as for Alejo Carpentier and other writers, the Machado dictatorship was a nightmare which would influence their subsequent literary expression and their treatment of the theme of dictatorship.[10]

By 1928, Machado was ready to enshrine himself in the Presidential office: he designated himself the "Illustrous and Exemplary Citizen", abolished the Vice Presidency, changed the Presidential term from four to six years and stood for re-election unopposed. The start of the new term in 1929 saw a rapid worsening of the national situation: intensified terrorism by Machado, the closing of the University of Havana and the Havana Yacht Club and the hardening of protest into violent resistance not only by students but by a new middle-class revolutionary group - the ABC - which took to bombings and shooting of police officers in retaliation against the Machado tyranny.

THE NINETEEN-THIRTIES

This led to the inevitable turbulent outburst in 1933. In December, 1932, the Confederación Nacional de Obreros Cubanos (CNOC) convened a Conference of sugar workers which prepared a strike involving over 20,000 workers, leaving only about 125 mills in operation. More opposition groups became actively engaged in anti-Machado protests - a new middle-class secret society, the Organización Celular Radical Revolucionaria (OCRR), and, high school teachers' and women's organizations, in particular. By August 1933, "Cuba presented a desolate and disconcerting picture; there were strikes in all service sections of Havana, with the railway workers out for the first time. Newspapers were also shutting down. The bars and cafés were closed for the first time in history. Food was scarce. Most shops were shut...there were no milk or ice deliveries". (Thomas, p. 615). The final straw came when negotiations between Machado and opposition groups under the army, led by Colonel Erasmo Delgado, joined the general demand for Machado's removal from power. The President was finally persuaded to take permanent leave of absence and surrender political control.

Then came a rapid succession of changes involving Carlos Manuel de Céspedes, Dr. Ramón Grau San Martín, the radical Dean of the Faculty of Medicine at the University of Havana, Carlos Hevia, Colonel Carlos Mendieta and the eloquent military stenographer Sergeant Fulgencio Batista who suddenly emerged at the forefront of national politics to dominate the turbulent years of revolt, strikes, scheming and treachery, from 1933 to 1940.

The year 1934 was particularly tumultous. In February, 30,000 tobacco workers struck. Then followed a series of strikes involving telephone workers, gas workers, water and tram-car workers, workers in sugar mills, students and even doctors and nurses. The frequency of riots, demonstrations and bombings was such that by march 7, 1934, Mendieta had to suspend constitutional guarantees. Continuing unrest and intermittent spurts of rioting forced Mendieta to suspend constitutional laws for another three months in January, 1935. A wide-spread strike involving government employees, public service workers, railway workers, the Communists, the ABC and the student activists brought President Mendieta to the point where a "state of siege" had to be declared on 10th March, 1935. By December, Mendieta was ready to resign and Batista's command of the military and his unofficial control of the country could no longer be doubted. He dominated the Senate, he controlled welfare services and the schools through his rural military agents and he influenced the Unions, baiting them with favorable labour legislation. He even won the confidence and support of the Communist leaders Juan Marinello and Carlos Rafael Rodríguez, as well as Blas Roca and Joaquín Ordoquí because of his welfare and educational programmes, his pretentious show of benevolence to potical exiles and prisoners in the amnesties declared in September 1936 and December 1937, in his avowed commitment to democracy, and his posture as "the socially conscious military ruler."[11]

The Unions also were won over by his provisions for insurance coverage, paid holidays, minimum wage, protection against unfair dismissal and various other benefits for workers. His plans for state control of the sugar and tobacco industries, for reforestation and reorganization of agriculture, for redistribution of state lands for mining and oil, for a merchant marine, for a new health plan and new water supply and for a new tax system and a new currency, were all indications of an impressive progressive thrust that made the closing years of that decade look like the era of greatest nationalist consciousness, national unity and national reconstruction, particularly after the turmoil and destruction of the preceding years. And yet, Guillén remained strongly critical of the role of the military in national politics.

THE NINETEEN-FORTIES

Aganist that background, reasonably fair elections were held for the Constituent Assembly in November, 1939 and for the Presidency in 1940. A new Constitution was drafted and adopted in 1940 and on October 10, Batista assumed duties as legally elected President, replacing his faithful figure-head President, Laredo Bru, who had held office since December, 1936. At the end of his four-year term, Batista withdrew gracefully and allowed Dr. Saladrijas, his Prime Minister, to stand as Presidential candidate. By this time, however, Dr. Grau San Martín was back in the foreground of national politics as the candidate of the Auténticos and he won the 1944 elections. Succeeding him in 1948 was Carlos Príon Socarrás, another product of the University of Havana and its body of political activists, and a close ally of Grau's since the thirties.

The administrations of this eight-year span from the 1944-52 proved to be no less corrupt and inept than proceeding ones. A split between Príon and Grau led to charges and counter-charges of corruption, inefficiency and mismanagement. Grau, in fact, ended up in the courts having been indicted by Prío's government. Political rivalry was upheld by intensified gangsterism: reprisals, murders, attacks on the courts by masked gunmen, open duels, gang warfare, and assassination of labour leaders (including the Negro leader Jesús Menéndez) and student activists.

Interestingly enough, this period of violence and corruption was also a period of prosperity for the middle classes. Cuba's sugar benefitted from the price increases during the Second World War and the Korean War and from the U.S. demands for more sugar particularly in their effort to asist Europe in their post-war recovery. New cars and television sets became the new symbols of wealth and prosperity for all but the poor. Grau had himself tried to help the working class people through his low-income housing schemes, rural school programme, and road improvement drive, but he left untouched more crucial issues such as land reform, crop diversification and rural development. Prío's administration was no better in so far as the interest and welfare of the poor were concerned. In fact, he was constantly faced with serious labour threats from dock workers, bus workers and rail workers. This was the period that marked Guillén's severest use of political satire as a Revolutionary weapon. It was this biting satire in 1949 and later in 1952-53 that caused him to have to live in exile between 1953 and 1959.

THE EVE OF REVOLUTION

By 1952, the country was ready for revolutionary change and, ironically, the man to whom they looked for relief was Colonel Batista who had been living outside of Cuba for several years since leaving office in 1944. Batista who had maintained a strong influence in Congress and the Senate during this time led a successful coup against the Príon government in March 1952 and immediately won the recognition and support of the U.S. government. This ushered in a seven-year period of highly refined and sophisticated totalitarianism, the last phase of the pre-Revolutionary Cuban saga. It was a period characterized by the suspension of constitutional rule, absolute muzzling of the Press and labour unions, persecution and assassination of students and political suspects, corruption in public administration, disaster in public finances and growing resistance by young revolutionaries.

The Republican era (1902-59) was a particularly nervous and explosive period of transition from the colonial experience to Revolutionary achievement. The prevailing social and political conditions provided a nursery for the moulding of young revolutionary spirits which grew increasingly disenchanted with the poverty and distress of the masses, the prosperity of the privileged classes, the terror and corruption of political operators and the over-bearing presence and influence of the United States in the economic and political affairs of the Republic.

THE U.S. PRESENCE

The extent to which the U.S. dominated Cuban politics and economy has always been a very sore point. Starting with the U.S. intervention in the independence war with Spain and the subsequent occupation of Cuba by U.S. forces during the four years prior to the establishment of Republican status, resentment to the U.S. presence has grown steadily during the twentieth century. The actual dominance of the U.S. commerical interests was exemplified in the presence of: The Trust Co. of Cuba, the Houston Contracting Co., United Fruit Co., The Ports Co., Atlantic Sugar Co. of the Gulf, the Cuban American Co., Punta Alegre Co., American Sugar Refining Co., Cuban Cane Co., Cuban Trading Co., West Indies Finance Corporation, Bank of Nova Scotia, North American Trust Co. (National Bank of Cuba), Cuban Central Railway Ltd., Cuban Eastern Railroad, Jaraguá Iron Co., The Sigua Iron Co., Spanish American Iron Co., Bethlehem Iron Works, Ponupo Manganese Co., National City Bank, American Foreign Banking Corporation, Mercantile Bank of America and Guaranty Trust Co.[12]

The American presence in Cuba when coupled with the facts of American intervention in Panama, Guatemala, Haiti, Santo Domingo, Nicaragua, Puerto Rico, etc., provoked writers like Guillén to raise virulent strains of protest. However, in the meantime, more deeply personal things were happening to Guillén, for whom the period 1937-1940 were particularly challenging years.

PERSONAL EXPERIENCE

The young progressive mulatto of promising liberal leanings began to show clearer signs of leftist leanings around 1934 when he began to associate with the left wing press. When, in 1937, he was officially admitted to the Communist Party, he was taking a step which would intensify the drama of his personal life and sharpen his perception of his role as a poet in Republican Cuba. The tenor of his poetry in his soldier poems of 1937 indicates the clarity of his understanding of this evolution from a liberal parental background to an ideologically Revolutionary stance vis-a-vis the Republic which had shaped his destiny and his political conscience.

It is significant that his formal admission to the Communist Party took place in Valencia in 1937 in the heat of the Spanish Civil War, for the war contributed profoundly to the sharpening of his personal Revolutionary focus. Once he returned to Cuba, the poet who had previously shunned politics, in spite of his father's active role in provincial politics and in the Senate, suddenly became persuaded to accept nomination for candidacy as Mayor of Camagüey in the 1940 general elections.

Guillén, around 1921-22, had been a close friend and assocaite of the radical young poet and intellectual Rubén Martínez Villena who developed into one of Cuba's leading Communist organizers in the late twenties. In August 1922, after completing only the first year in the Faculty of Law at the University of Havana he quit studies and took to the bohemian life for a period of about 4 years. He was twenty years old then. His departure from the University was marked by his writing of a small collection of sonnets entitled "Al margen de mis libros de estudio" which revealed his boredom and disappointment with University life. Yet he never got involved in the violent demonstrations against the incompetence and corruption of lecturers in 1922. He was familiar with the revolutionary spirit and activities of young radicals like Julio Antonio Mella, the student who laid the base for the Communist Party in Cuba, or young white writers such as Alejo Carpentier, Jorge Mañach, etc. who were youngsters of his age actively engaged in open revolutionary activity against dictatorship and corruption in national politics. Yet he was not stirred to action along those lines until his return from Spain in 1938. Then, again, in 1948, on his return from a two-and-a-half year sojurn in South America he accepted nomination as candidate to the Senate.

The Guillén of the twenties was clearly still unsure of himself and his calling but the realities of his environment were gradually influencing his character and his consciousness. His association with Negro Societies in Camagüey which worked for the defense of Negro rights in Cuba nurtured what seems to have been an inchoate awareness of the real worth of the Negro contribution to the national identity. His journalism of 1928-1931 reflects the growth of that awareness into a firm position that drew him into controversy on the questions of race, culture and identity.

Even the mild sonnets of 1922 suddenly emerged around 1932 as the focus of further controversy when the journalist Sergio Carbó reproduced them in the newspaper, La Semana, under the title, "El caso terrible de Nicolás Guillén". They became the basis for Carbó's bitter attack on the Secretary for Education, General Alemán. Now, once more Guillén found himself at the center of a public debate which was broadening the controversy that was stirred up by his own newspaper writings on race, his protest poetry in Motivos de son and his poetic statement on Cuban culture in Sóngoro Cosongo. From here on, the nineteen-thirties witnessed the solid development and maturing of a political vision.

The first sign of the political activist's appearance came in August, 1936 when he was sacked from his Civil Service job and jailed for a few days for "subversive and pornographic writing" and anti-Government demonstrations. It is at this stage (1936-38) that the controversial figure was recognized by reactionary quarters as being more than a "mere poet" and black journalist. He became a threat and serious activist.

By 1938 he was a member of the National Committee of the Communist Revolutionary Union, and in 1941 he was denied a visa to go to the United States for a writers' conference. In 1949 he actually set foot on American soil (in New York) in transit to Paris, but he was arrested and held at Ellis Island and released the next day. In 1952, he was arrested twice by the Military Intelligence Service in Cuba and his passport confiscated. When he was finally allowed to leave in 1953, he was forced into exile by the Batista regime. Venezuela refused him a visa in 1958 and French immigration authorities in Paris arrested him for not having a valid passport. He eventually reached Argentina in mid-1958 and returned to Cuba on January 23, 1959, three weeks after Castro's successful coup.

Without perhaps even having to hold a rifle, Nicolás Guillén has established himself as one of the leading political activists of pre-Revolutionary Cuba and surely one of the most outstanding exponents of the Revolutionary philosophy of Castro's era.

There has been much controversy over the question of his ideological position on the question of race and racial prejudice in Cuba, negritude in Cuba and the wider Caribbean and his concept of a mulatto culture as a de facto Cuban inheritance. Much has been said about his treatment of the theme of Revolution and Marxist-Leninist influence on the tenor of his poetry. Much too has been said of the simplicity and over-simplification of his poetry.

These brief comments are intended to be one contribution to an on-going critical evaluation of one of the Caribbean's most distinguished poets who addresses himself specifically to the questions of Caribbean history and the evolution of a Caribbean experience under colonialism and imperialism as well as the particularities of society, race and culture in this Caribbean experience.

NOTES

[1] R. Scheer and M. Zeitland, CUBA: An American Tragedy, 1964, p. 37 - "The Government of Cuba consents that the United States may excercise the right to intervene for the preervation of Cuban independence the maintenance of a government adequate for the protection of life, property, and individual liberty, and for discharging the obligations with respect to Cuba imposed by the Treaty of Paris on the United States, now to be assumed and undertaken by the Government of Cuba.
To enable the United States to maintain the independence of Cuba, and to protect the people thereof, as well as for its own defence, the Cuban Government will sell or lease the United States and land neccessary for coaling or naval stations, at certain specified points, to be agreed uopn with the President of the United States."

[2] Hugh Thomas, CUBA or the Pursuit of Freedom (London, 1971) p. 442.

[3] Ibid. p. 417.

[4] R. Scheer and M. Zeitland, op. cit., pp. 36-37.

[5] Senado, Memoria, 1902-1904, cited in Hugh Thomas, CUBA.... , op. cit. p. 454.

[6] Julio Le Riverand, Economic History of Cuba, (Havana, 1967) p. 206.

[7] Hugh Thomas, CUBA...... op. pp. 418-419.

[8] Ibid. pp. 430-432.

[9] Ibid. p. 450.

[10] Carpentier was actually imprisoned in 1927 for alleged subversive activities against Macado. Up to this time, Guillén, unlike Carpentier was not yet branded as a communist. In fact, his position in the late twenties seems to have become more of a "progressive", liberal one which gradually became more firmly committed to social change

particularly during the traumatic years of 1933-34.

[11] Hugh Thomas, op. cit., p. 707.

[12] Julio Le Riverand, op. cit. pp. 216-225 and Hugh Thomas, op. cit. pp. 506-7 and 536-7.

CHAPTER TWO

GROWTH OF A REVOLUTIONARY CONSCIOUSNESS

A contemporary of Guillén's, Alberto Lamar Schweyer, in 1931, said of the young poet, "Nicolás Guillén is the revelation...(he) is Cuban in body and soul...And when the attempt is made to sketch history of our poetic evolution and many names shall fade away into silence, drowned in the mediocrity of their work and in the poverty of their creation, the name of Nicolás Guillén will remain".[1]

It was not a mere superfluous or gratuitous gesture then on the part of the Revolutionary Cuban Government to honour Guillén as Cuba's National Poet. It was an acknowledgement of an image of the poet which has evolved out of his contribution to and articulation of a national consciousness betweeen 1927 and the present. Guillén consistently played the role of the poet as the nation's conscience and the people's visionary. His sensibility has been like a screen on which the inner world of the nation and the intimacies of its soul have been bared. He was not just a mirror reflecting static reality, nor an onlooker-critic making detached observations. He was the nation's living conscience imbued with the guilt-tinged memories, the anxieties, anguish, rage and dreams of a people whose checkered and complex history has given rise to a whirlpool of conflicting feelings, attitudes and postures. It is a conscience that captures the intense social drama of the tumultous experience of the Republican era (1902-59), but which also attempts to look back through personal intuitions to respond to the history that produced that dilemma.

In fact, a distinct three-tiered socio-politicxal trajectory can be traced in his poetry from the time he resumed writing around 1927. The preiod 1927-1933 can be seen as the phase of "Social and Cultural Awakening"; 1934-1958 as the phase of "Political Activism" and 1959 onwards as the phase of "Revolutionary Consolidation".

SOCIAL AND CULTURAL AWAKENING:

The notion of the saturated conscience informed by and nurtured in the substance of its environment is one which he himself has expounded repeatedly. In his poem, "La voz desconocida", published in 1927, he speaks of a voice that is different from what one normally hears, one which is like a blow that is not heard but which is felt vibrating in the deepest regions of one's sensibility. What he is dealing with here is no doubt a psychological and spiritual pehenomenon which underpins his own growing sensitivity to injustice and suffering:

> It gives me a strange emotion
> wild, rudimentary,
> to witness blows from afar
> or blows which can't be heard,
> and feel them fall inside me
> vibrating as if in my ear.[2]

This position is reinforced in his poem "Elegía moderna del motivo cursi" (1931) in which he shuns the ethereal and romantic in favour of terrestrial and human realities not as posturing but as a means of coming to terms with life:

> I don't know what you think, brother, but I believe
> in educating the Muse from early in a
> genuine phobia against things of the Moon...
> ...Train it in the parks...
> let it sweat and box and get excited and vibrate
> let it bet at the races and play hand ball...
> ...my muse is already fashioned in my style.
> It smokes. It dances. It laughs. It knows a little law,
> it's varied in the sad community of the bed
> and sweet when I shout, blaspheme and get vexed.[3]

His definitive exposition on the subject is given in the following extract:

> There is nothing in this base world -not even
> poetry-
> which is free from the circumstances in which it is
> produced. Is it perhaps that a "pure" poet fails to
> reflect in his work (which he thinks is esoteric and

> distant) the formation of his nature, the material moulding of his spirit by the immediate realities which intervene in his education. And the same thing happens with the "impure" ones (among whom I am pleased to include myself) who speak of the beings around them; of men and women who walk along the street or visit the cinema, or stand at counters in fish markets, or on platforms, who travel in trains, speak on the telephone, eat or fornicate. How can one maintain that the poet's orbit is a free uncontaminated one, and that his destiny is above that of all other men who walk on earth?[4]

When *Motivos de son* was published in 1930, it grew out of that nascent consciousness of the social moorings of the poet and therefore assumed the full import of a clear political statement (however rudimentary) on the state of the nation which could produce and embosom the tragedy of the ghetto without pangs of conscience.

Sónogoro Cosongo, in 1931, addressed itself directly to a nation's troubled conscience over the delicate questions of national identity and racial and cultural heritage; but it also captured the nation's incipient guilt-complex over the gravity of the threat of U.S. imperialism in Cuba. The poet who is responding to the culture of the folk in "Pregón", "Quirino", "Secuestro de la mujer de Antonio", "Canto negro", "Rumba", "Mujer nueva", "Madrigal" and "Velorio de Papá Montero", is equally alert to the social dilemmas raised in "Llegada", "La canción del bongo", "Chéverre" and "Oraganillo". But his response grows sharp and biting when he is facing the political and economic realities of U.S. exploitation. In both "Caña" and "Pequeña oda a un negro boxeador cubano"his comment is the terse and incisive image of a kind of "sugar soucayant", that drains the nation's life-blood:

> The North is fierce and rude, boxer.
> That same Broadway,
> is the one which stretches its snout with its enormous
> moist tongue,
> to lick up like a glutton
> all the blood of our sugar.[5]

In fact, this poem had been anteceded by "Futuro" in 1927 where the poet condemns those Americans "who humiliate us with their strength."[6]

POLITICAL ACTIVISM

West Indies Ltd., in 1934, broadens and deepens the ambit of this social conscience as it goes beyond the issues of racial prejudices and explores the undercurrents of suffering and protest on the docks and the streets ("Nocturno en los muelles", "Sabás", "Caminando" and "Canción de los hombres perdidos"), or in the bars and the brothels ("Balada de Simón Caraballo" and "West Indies Ltd.": #4). It examines the riddles and paradoxes of national life as they relate to issues such as the place of the Negro, the ownership of sugar and the faces of hunger and begging, in "Adivinanzas".

Even the folklore poems ("Madrigal", "Balada del güije", "Maracas" and "Sensemayá") seem to embody some deeply personalized response to the socio-political environment. "Madrigal" cannot be seen merely as a sensual response to a woman; it also seems to be an indirect comment on the rapacious eye that covets the tempting taste of sugar. In that event, the images of "equine foam/scum", "shouting spasm" and "metal thighs" take on significant industrial and materialistic meanings that are hidden behind suggestive sexual concepts.

Similarly, "Sensemaya" cannot be restricted to its usual folkloric interpretation drawn straight from the santería cult. In the same way that "Maracas" deals specifically with the question of varying levels of consciousness about the Cubans' relationship with the U.S. tourist dollar, "Sensemayá" must have something to say about the serpentine and sinuous inroads being made by the U.S. into the Cuban economy and national life. The extended image of the glassy-eyed "snake in the grass" that should not be kicked, but killed, does more than merely evoke a folk ritual. It conjures up the ritual defeat of imperialism and exploitation through the popular faith and collective energy and effort of the people.

In like manner, "Balada del güije", is more than a mere cradle song that captures popular faith and superstitions of the folk. The portentous and mysterious air of exorcism has to do with more than the purging of river sprites, imagined goblins and demon-possessed men. It is dealing with real devils, economic devils that suck the blood of the child/nation, hideous devils that cross the waters to mutilate the sapling nation and leave it with dry veins, toothless gums and a bare skeleton of knotted bones. When the poem ends on the note, "I told you so!", it does not signify a dead end; it still leaves open the possibility that the devil might still be exorcised.

Even the poem, "Palabras en el trópico", raises serious political questions relating to the Caribbean region in general. Here the poet's concern is extended and deepened to respond to a common regional destiny, so that his salute to the Tropics is made on behalf of a family of islands which are like "scandalous little daughters" romping with bare buttocks in the Caribbean sea, and revelling in a kind of child-like enthusiasm for the simple things of life,

while a maritime heaven
splinters itself in endless waves of stars at (their) feet.[7]

Whether this can be seen as a possible allusion to the stars and stripes and the marines occupying local territory has to be evaluated in relation to the "lizard/ alligator anguish" referred to earlier in the same poem.

It is the title poem, "West Indies Ltd.", that crystallizes best the political thrust of this phase of Guillén's writing. It has to be interpreted against the background of: the Machado dictatorship, and the frustrations of the workers' struggle in the face of the combined efforts of Machado and his supporters from U.S. political, diplomatic and commercial circles; the persecution of progressive elements that opposed Machado and protested the scale of U.S. investments in Cuba; the extent of corruption in local politics and administration; the increase in tourism in the entire Caribbean region in the 1920's and 1930's and its impact on the social attitudes, cultural life and social ills of the region, the facts of U.S. intervention in Central America (Mexico, Honduras, Nicaragua and Panamá) and a visible U.S. military presence in Haiti (1915-34), Santo Domingo (1916-30), Cuba and Puerto Rico; and the effective stronghold of the U.S. on Caribbean sugar industries and banking.

The dominant note of the poem is its emphasis on the theme of rebellion over and above a mere note of protest. What started out in "Sabás" as a call to renounce begging and submissiveness and to demand, with hope and confidence, the livelihood which was his right, develops in "Nocturno en los muelles" into a dream of change symbolized by the image of the beacon "shouting" across the dark sea. The basis of this hope rests in a "non-conformist spirit" that bursts forth and which, in "Canción de los hombres perdidos" takes on a strong militant character, as hungry men don their masks and the symbolic gorilla leaps from his tight-rope with the cry:

Take courage, friends! Loosen up your legs,
Sharpen your teeth, harden your snout,
and don't get dizzy going around in circles!
Let us hurl ourselves on the city.
Like abandoned dogs
in the heart of a storm![8]

Now, in "West Indies Ltd." this rebellion becomes a symbolic Revolutionary song that emanates spontaneously from the depths of the people's anguish; but it is a song whose message is charcterized by "elasticity" and which therefore has the potential to stretch out in time and space to embrace sugar workers and other exploited workers across the Caribbean. It acknowledges that there are many who are incapable of reading the signs of the times ("the blind who live but do not see when the sun comes out") and who cannot perceive the dawning of a new day, but it also posits that "heads will fly" when the Revolutionaries begin to cut off heads like sugarcane,[9] and win their hard-earned liberty.[10]

In his *Cantos para soldados* (1937) this Revolutionary spirit solidifies into action. The military-capitalist alliance is being undermined as soldiers in the lower ranks begin to recognize their true enemy and return to their natural alliance with the working class. The ugly face of fascism is unveiled whether it is in Abyssinia or in Cuba and the result is the clarion call, in "Diana" (reveille), for a proletarian rebellion which would inevitably include the ghetto characters in the *Sones para turistas* (1937).

España: Poema en cuatro angustias y una esperanza takes up the themes of Fascism and the popular resistance in Spain and links them with the Cuban situation in 1937 just as *El soldado Miguel Paz y el sargento José Inés* (1952) links the Korean struggle of the late nineteen forties with the Cuban struggle in *Coplas de Juan Descalzo* (1952-1953), or in *Sátira política* (1949). The panorama is widened but the perspective remains the same. This period 1937-53 marks the consolidation of the poet's revolutionary vision and his interpretation of the movement of his people towards the 1953 Moncada attack, the 1956 "Granma" landing and the 1959 coup that proved to be the fulfillment of their dreams and aspirations.

El son entero (1947) might seem like a mild interpolation in this revolutionary development which was progressively becoming more and more intense, but its value is not to be overlooked. Its main contributions to the process are: its statement on the value of the *"son"* as a popular instrument for protest and an organ for capturing the hopes of the people for revolutionary change ("Guitarra"); its comment on the dialectical nature of the people's evolution towards an "open future" ("Mi patria es dulce por fuera".....and "Sudor y Látigo"); its suggestion that change requires violence either in the slaying of the vicious American marines ("Mi patria es dulce por fuera.....") or in the spilling of the master's blood ("Sudor y Látigo"); its reiteration of the need for solidarity among people of all races (Son número 6); the linking of the U.S. presence in Colombia, Venzuela and the rest of the mainland to the situation in Cuba ("Son Venezolano", "Barlovento", "Una canción en el Magdalena"); and the open expression of the Communist role in the liberation movement ("Una canción a Stalín).

The *Elegías* (1958) bridge the gap between 1953 and 1959, the period of the poet's exile. "Elegía cubana" captures the full weight and significance of the maturing of the people's revolutionary spirit - a deep sense of national anguish over the long history of colonialism and imperialism, which the poet perceives as he descends

to the angry abyss
of (their) untiring and precipitous chest...
where he
feels

every heartbeat
like a sea in diastole
like a sea in systole
like a concentric sea..."[11]

What he senses is a deep uneasiness of spirit which he describes as "the lugubrious throbbing of sleepless water" which symbolizes the sighs, hopes and aspirations of his prototypes - Juan Dezcalzo, Juan Montuno, Juan Negro, Juan Blanco and Juan Pueblo. The poem finally assumes prophetic proportions when it suggests that a "child hero" would take up the old struggle, "armed with his own brilliance" and would fulfil the dreams of the people in the name of Martí and Maceo. The events of Moncada (1953) and Granma (1956) were only to confirm the extent to which the poet had accurately understood his people's pulse in 1952.

"Elegía a Jesús Menéndez", in capturing the feverish intensity of the workers' struggle against repression, becomes a fitting climax to poems such as: "Balada de Simón Caraballo" in which the protest singer is silenced by repressive military forces; "Fusilamiento", where misguided soldiers assassinate his father, and like him, many others who define the military-capitalist-imperialist alliance in Cuba; and "West Indies Ltd." which establishes the regional nature of the people's struggle for liberation from imperialist domination.

The assassination of Menéndez is seen as a useful yardstick for measuring the progress of the people's movement and an appropriate gauge for the growing tensions and fears among the oppressors. It is a significant local index of the internal weaknesses of the political structure in the nineteen-forties that led to the eventual coup by Batista in 1952; but it is also an indicator of the growing awareness of the regional and continental domensions of the Cuban class dilemma. The poet gets his finger into the sore spot of the nation and of the region when he places all these issues in their true historical-economic perspective. The work and dreams of Jesús Menéndez are not personal, but collective and proletarian, not insular but regional, linked concretely and historically with: Dessalines and Jacques Roumain in Haiti; Puerto Rican captives chained in American neo-colonialism; Central America under the agony of the United Fruit Co.; Venezuelan oil workers in Zulia "curdled in fat oil"; Chilean saltpetre workers in Tarapacá and Tocopilla; Negro coffee and banana workers and boatmen in Colombia; as well as Mexican Indian *peones*, Brazilian *favelas* and Peruvian silver mines.

The death of Jesús Menéndez is treated as a historic milestone in the people's evolution and a symbolic sacrifice that points towards eventual victory. Guillén chooses to counterpoint him with Jesus Christ. The Cuban Jesús makes no promises, he does not go off to heaven, he builds no churches, he solicits no prayers, he recruits no priests. He stays on earth, organizes workers' Unions, attracts working companions, calls for struggle, and even when he is silent, all the oppressed inside and outside of Cuba see "in his eyes the splendor of an abundant promise" and regard his powerful revolutionary fist as their guide. The symbolic pigeon with its green olive branch is introduced as a messenger of hope and freedom for a people who are in the final stages of struggle,

> the final procession, the vast entourage
> of victory.[12]

La paloma de vuelo popular (1958) now leaves no stones unturned. Protests against repression in all it forms - police brutality, political imprisonment, denial of visas and passports and political exile are strongly expressed in "Policía", "Doña María", "Pero Señor", "Exilio", "Paloma del palomar" and "Hacia el Paraguay lejano". Protest against exploitation, foreign occupation and domination whether by the English in Africa or the U.S. in this region is also denounced: "Mau Maus", "Ciudades", "Canción Puertorriqueña", "A Guatemala", "Balada Guatemalteca", "Casa de vecindad", "Cañaveral", and "El banderón." Protest against continued suffering among the proletariat and a note of solidarity with the dispossessed emerge in "Canción carioca", "Bares", "Rios", "La muralla", "Canción de vísperas", "Canción de cuna para desperter a un negrito" and "Arte poética". Then a firm position is taken on the validity and strategic value of violence as a part of the people's struggle: "Little Rock" and "Pequeña letanía grotesca por la muerte del senador McCarthy."

As 1959 approaches, the poet's vision gets clearer, his heart more hopeful and his voice more prophetic. "El banderón" foretells the defeat of the American flag on Cuban soil; "Casa de vecindad" forsees the sacrifice of a "Bloody future" heralded by "a simple song of life and death" and "unleashed dream"; and "Un largo lagarto verde" prefigures the need for watchfulness after the rude awakening of the Revolution. Who will be the watch-dogs - the Americans protecting their interests or the Cubans defending their Revolution? The answer is wide open depending on the side of 1959 from which one looks at the poem.

REVOLUTIONARY CONSOLIDATION

G.R. Coulthard once said of *Tengo* (1964): *"Tengo*, to a large extent, is a rehash of his earlier works, with more emphasis on the Anti-American angle. Much of what he writes had already been written in *West Indies Ltd.*"[13] Lloyd King elsewhere says of Guillén's poetry: "Guillén has worn the mask of an Afro-cuban poet as part of his role as a protest writer...but his poetry has not expanded in any important way since 1934 when he published his best poem, "West Indies Ltd."[14]

If one chooses to assess Guillén only in terms of his role as "Mr. Black in Cuba", then King's statement can well be deemed to have some measure of validity. And yet, Guillén's treatment of the Negro theme *per se*, outside of Cuba, is one area in which there has been some recognizable broadening of concerns. Poems such as "U.S.A.", "Elegía a Till", "Little Rock", "Un negro canta en Nueva York", "Angela Davis", "Qué color?" and "Está bién" represent an important phase of Guillén's poetry that has no direct forerunners in the pre-1934 phase. His specific concern for the plight of the Negro in the heart of the U.S. "democratic Republic" marks a significant change from the down-playing of the racial theme in Cuba to a virulent revival of the question of race as a major aspect of the proletarian struggle within the United States.

But the real compass of Guillén's work cannot be measured purely by its focus on race. The more important and, in fact, the overriding interest is the question of the Revolutionary pursuit of change for the benefit of all humanity. It is the broad human concern that gives his poetry its undoubted depth of perception and breadth of appeal.

If his poetry up to *La paloma de vuelo popular* (1958) delineates an evolution towards revolutionary commitment to change, then *Tengo* (1964) celebrates the achievement of that change, and the poetry subsequent to *Tengo* enunciates the consolidation of that Revolutionary achievement. *Tengo* fulfils several useful roles. From the vantage point of a successful Revolution, the poem "Vine en un barco negrero" looks back on the historical landscape as far back as the slave ships and charts the progressive march towards freedom: slave ship, sugar, whip, stocks, sun, sweat; Aponte, the Nineteenth century rebellious slave leader; Maceo, the black national hero of the independence war; Jesús Menéndez, the Negro trade unionist; all slain for their defense of justice and their call for freedom. The Negro within the Revolution is proud of that history:

> I am free, I came a long way
> I am a Negro.[15]

"Allá lejos" takes a shorter backward glance of fifty years towards the early days of American infiltration - days of the "Platt Amendment, armed intervention and battleships", the cultural invasion, the commercial enterprises and the monopolies - and captures the gradual disillusionment of the people and their final awakening to the real advantages of Revolutionary change.

Tengo also monitors the country's continued distrust and condemnation of U.S. imperialism in all forms: "Bonsal" deals with the U.S. Ambassador, Phillip Bonsal whom the Cubans view as a traitor to the Revolutionary movement because of his opposition to the Agrarian Reform programme; "Marines U.S.A." condemns the "Yankee-pirates in the Caribbean Sea" for their attempts at invasion; "Frente al Oxford" deals with the warships posted at the entrance to Havana harbour as a watchdog for the U.S. blockade of Cuba, and decries the sacrilege of U.S. marines who had urinated on Martí's statue in Havana's Central Park in 1949; "Crecen altas las flores" criticizes the U.S. Alliance for Progress introduced by John F. Kennedy as a means of arresting Cuban influence in Latin America; "Coplas americanas" analyses U.S. imperialism throughout Latin America and the resistance movements it provokes; "Las dos cartas" deals with the Cuban reply to the famous "Carta/ declaración de San José" when the O.A.S. yielded to U.S pressure to ostracize Cuba in February, 1960.

Tengo futher serves as a chronicle of the Revolutionary process in Cuba after 1959: "Tierra en la sierra y el llano" deals with the Agrarian Reform initiated early in 1959; "Se acabó" records the people's joy at the final blow dealt to U.S. imperialism with the nationalization of American industries in Cuba in 1960; "Soy como un árbol florido" looks at the literacy campaign and its reciprocal educational effects; "Letrilla cubana", and "Son del bloqueo" were written during the October Crisis of 1962 in the face of impending U.S. invasion; "Responde tú" deals with the exodus of the reactionaries, challenging those natives who deserted their homeland after the Revolution.

In clear tones of exultation and idealism, *Tengo* celebrates the joys and successes of the Revolution: the title poem"Tengo" looks back to contrast the old days of class prejudice and discrimination with the egalitarianism of the present; "Cualquier tiempo pasado fue peor" marks the dramatic social transformation brought about by the Revolution; "Canta el sinsonte en el Turquino" and "Mister No" say farewell to the U.S. presence that had plagued that society and revel in the joys of a newly found freedom; "Nadie" expresses the newly found confidence of the people, in a way that is similar to the expression of pride in "Puedes?" where they have regained full control of Cuban territory and their real birthright.

It also registers the heroism of the actual physical struggle in the sierra, and the clandestine struggle in the city ("Muchacha recién crecida") prior to 1959. However, "La sangre numerosa" salutes the symbolic act of heroism of a young soldier, Eduardo García, who was wounded during the U.S. bombings of Cuban airports and bases that prepared the way for the Bay of Pigs invasion in April, 1961. García, just before dying wrote a significant page in Cuban history by using his own blood to write the name Fidel on one of the walls of the building in which he was wounded. Other poems such as "Mella", "Martí" and "Se acabó" link the triumph of the Revolution with the foundations laid by José Martí and Julio Antonio Mella who had themselves written heroic pages in the history of the revolutionary movements. "Romancero" extols the heroism of Fidel Castro and his men from the landing of the Granma up to the U.S. blockade.

The ideological direction of the Revolution is interestingly suggested in the poems "Lenin" and "Unión Soviética", whereas the Latin American thrust for transferring the Revolution to the mainland countries is unreservedly enunciated in "Brasil-Copacabana: Telón", "A Chile", "A Colombia" and "Panamá."

The variety of forms and voices with which the poet speaks in *Tengo* (songs, sones, elegy, satire, dialogue, ballads) and the range of themes he treats could be, in themselves, an adequate answer to Coulthard's criticism. Better than any of the young poets or even the prose writers of the Revolutionary era, Guillén has absorbed the braod popular responses to the early days of anxiety, confrontation, excitement, elation and discovery. Whereas other writers convey their personal responses to the crises of the sixties - Bay of Pigs, U.S. Blockade, October Crises or Caribbean Crises (U.S. - U.S.S.R. confrontation), O.A.S. ban, etc. - or to national challenges - cane-cutting, literacy campaign, Escambray struggle etc. - Guillén dedicated his poetry to the definition and pronouncement of national issues, national concerns and a national point of view. That is the real value of *Tengo* in the overall spectrum of Guillén's Revolutionary stance and vision.

The collections of poetry that follow *Tengo* mark the phase of Revolutionary consolidation. *El gran zoo* (1967) extols the virtues of the Revolution and its achievements through an abstruse and ironic approach. The book seems to constitute a critical and meditative reflection on the contemporary world situation from the vantage point of the Cuban Revoultion. The Universe is reduced to the size of a zoo and particular human characters, natural phenomena and social realities are symbolically and metaphorically dealt with as animals on show. The very first poem, "Aviso" makes it clear that the Cuban poet and the Cuban people with their new Revolutionary awakening, their sharpened sensibility and perception and their enlightened outlook on the world at large assume the role of the readers' guide through the microcosmic zoo, and significantly, at the end of the tour, the arrow points towards a "leftist" exit and path.

The tones are readily perceivable - joy, pride, amusement, concern, distaste, sarcasm, mimicry - and the themes reminiscent of things encountered before, but brought into critical focus. "Institutriz" immediately reminds one of "Frente al

Oxford", but couched in terms of the lesson the people have learnt from the experience of the blockaade; "Lynch" and "KKK" return to the Negro theme in the context of U.S. racism but pointing towards the eventual frustration and destruction of white terrorism by either castration or starvation; "La osa mayor" presents the old theme of the unbridled greed and ambition of imperailists who seek to conquer outer space perhaps because they can no longer hunt on Cuban soil; "Tonton-Macoute" and "Gorilla" recall earlier denunciation of Fascism and military dictatorship characterized here as sub-human, primitive and barbaric types of the quadruped family who are still lower on the evolutionary scale than monkeys; "El cangrejo" and "Gangster" are located "on the right", right-wing types in association, no doubt, acting like both crab and destructive cancer, but whose days are numbered; and "Oradores", "Tenor", "Policía" and "Monos" revive the old satirical vein with the full force of caricature and mimicry.

Some old themes are taken out of the previously limited and localized context and reviewed on the basis of their universal import. The theme of hunger which ran through his poetry from *Motivos de son* onwards, reappears with the same hideous face it had in "Balada de Simón Caraballo", "Canción de los hombres perdidos", "Sabás", "Adivinanzas", "Barlovento" and "West Indies Ltd.", but it is no longer a Cuban dilemma. It is a universal phenomenon that will raise its revoultionary head in due course in different parts of the world. Similarly, the U.S. eagle and its imperialist symbolism is placed squarely in a universal, historic perspective that embraces Roman, German, Austrian and Napoleonic versions of the same game, as well as certain astronomical/astrological, commercial and economic implications, while "La sed" seems to issue a warning against the universal phenomenon of greed and rapine.

In the context of that universal situation, the Caribbean experience is instructive. The Caribbean is just one little "animal" in an aquarium, in one small corner of the great zoo, but it possesses tremendously explosive potential which could have resounding effects on the world scene. The Cuban Revolution has provided ample evidence of this, hence the poems, "El Caribe" and "La guitarra".

The sensual overtones of "señora" carry a message of vicious rape followed by convalèscence which could well be subserved by an alternate message of national recovery after the ravages of the pre-Revolutionary era. If this is so, it is a preview of the message of the "Prólogo" of *La rueda dentada* (1972) which Keith Ellis interprets as "a parable, an extended metaphoor, carrying a message aimed at facilitating the process of reconstruction".[16]

The issue goes further than that however. The process of reconstruction and consolidation is the main burden of the book, *La rueda dentada*, and not just of the introductory poem. In fact, the sonnet dedicated "to a friend proposing reconciliation" is more than a personal settlement; it is a symbolic restoration of harmony, an attempt at accommodation, appeasement, propitiation and even expiation in the interest of national wholeness through reunion. On the basis of this principle of reconciliation and rediscovery of wholeness and national integration, the poet leads the reader into an exploration of attitudes and values that must form the sediment and substance of the new society.

The poem "Cosmonauta" may have something to do with space exploration, but it also has to do with the theme of human progress and the explosion of myths and structures that once plagued the society. The space explorer is significantly not an astronaut; he is a cosmonaut using science and progress in the service of humanity and not for destruction of the magnitude of Hiroshima. The God in question is not necessarily only the Christian God, but may well be the imperialist "god" who has been unseated. The breaking of the veil and the discovery of space speak of the rupture of old mental, political and economic structures, the unmasking of myths about the invincibility of world super-powers and the discovery of a new expansiveness in freedom. The poem also speaks of religious hierarchies and perhaps social stratifications that are denuded as the symbolic cosmonaut ascends, that is, as the people themselves rise towards open space, an open future and an expansive destiny. The poem, "Burgueses" amply supports this concern for consolidating the new social order without qualms or misgivings. "

?Qué color?" seems not to be a poem concerned primarily with blackness or whiteness as racial concepts. It is hardly likely that Guillén would be defending blackness of soul for a black man, or denying him the whiteness of soul attributed to King by Evtuchenko on purely racial grounds. His position on the cultural and spiritual interfaces in the white/black mixtures of the New World is too firm to admit any such racial implications. The crucial question must then be one of consistency of character and the rejection of duplicity, pretence and hypocrisy. Man must be on the inside what he appears to be on the outside and on the grounds of that integrity bring to human relations a "colourless", universal love. That seems also to be the sense of "Digo que yo no soy un hombre puro". Purity, to have any validity, must be a concept related to sincerity and integrity. In a Revolutionary context, particularly in an uncertain transitional period (perhaps 1959-68), such an interpretation is distinctly relevant.

"Problemas del subdesarrollo" and "Papel de tapizar" confront the question of values in the new society. The former deals with the rediscovery of self and self-image against the backdrop of labels created and imposed by foreign agents who see themselves as paradigms, and the latter deals a death-blow to capitalism and materialism in the new society as the dead money in all its millions becomes a mere ornament and a relic of the past.

"Noche de negros junto a la catedral" and "La herencia" underline two different attitudes. The first rejects superficial masquerading of historical issues and calls for a serious and perceptive interpretation of the dialectics of national history and the clash of interests and forces. The second proscribes the desertion of the mother-land by reactionary elements who pay no heed to the possible probings, dreams and ultimate destiny of their offspring, and seems to conclude that history will not absolve them.

In this context, the artist has a special role to play. To evade the immediate reality by way of flights to Paris, the Latin American artists' Mecca, or to waste time in imitation and fantasy, is to deprive the country of a voice it needs ("Paris"). Similarly, to spend one's energies on feudal trappings and the defense of old class interests is to lose an opportunity to come to grips with a world-wide struggle for justice ("Poetas"). That is the kind of awareness that commits itself to solidarity and optimism: solidarity with the people of Viet Nam ("Pequeña oda a Viet Nam"); solidarity with the Korean people ("En el museo de Pyong-yang"); and solidarity with the ideals, courage and strength of Angela Davis - solidarity without romantic or lascivious self-interest ("Angela Davis"). The "Rueda dentada" then is both a national and a universal symbol. The local process of national reconstruction is not to be ignored. The entire human circle is only as effective as its individual component parts.

The poem, "Victor Manuel", dedicated to the Cuban painter, Victor Maunel García (1897-1969), is an enlightening creation both for its message and its technique. It illustrates the process of reconstruction by using the words and ideas with which the poet starts in the first stanza, to experiment with a variety of formations. Words take on different forms, shades and positions in what seems to be a search for a definitive form, but the work remains integrated and unified and eventually arrives at an end product that seems to satisfy the search for answers.

In *El diario que a diario* (1972) the poet and the society have arrived at a point in the Revolutionary experience where they can look back at the long, hard journey from colony to Revolution. It traces the inhumanities and materialistic motives that inspired those atrocities from the time of the conquest and the early period:

> Those early days
> in which life was paid for in pesos and reales,
> and when not, with lashes from cable-laid rope whips;
> and from the crotch of cheap women
> fell the fruits of the rude cannon shots
> given by masters in heat
> loaded with hormones
> on beds and bunks, not forgetting the ground,
> to Negro slaves and mulatto women.[17]

He looks critically at the Anglo-Saxon nightmare started around 1762 with the arrival of the English expedition that defeated Don Juan Prado de Portocarrero and continued by their American dissidents in the late nineteenth century. He looks at the deplorable enslavement of whites and blacks alike and then underscores the French influence of the nineteenth century and the U.S. domination of the first half of the twentieth century. The tone is bitingly satirical, the technique is a varied and compelling blend of the cold, impersoanl style of posters, advertisement cards, newspaper clippings and the lively, personal note of cyncism and ridicule.

The net effect of this last work is a panoramic view of the events, conditions and forces that led up to the Cuban Revolution, the conflict of interests between the mass of the people and the privileged few and the nature of the society which moulded a poet to articulate its agonies and joys.

NOTES

[1]. Alberto Lamar Schweyer, "La musa mulata", Recopilacíon de textos sobre Nicolás Guillén Ed. Nancy Morejón, La Habana CASA, 1972, p. 255.

[2]. Nicolás Guillén, Obra poética 1920-1958, Vol. I, Instituto cubano del libro, La Habana, 1972, ed. Angel Augier, p. 86.

[3]. Ibid. p. 98-99.

[4]. Quoted by Angel Augier in Nicolás Guillén. Notas para un estudio biográfico-crítico, Vol. II, La Habana, Universidad Central de las Villas, 1962, pp. 153-154.

[5]. Guilleen, op. cit. pp. 118-119.

[6]. Ibid. p. 88.

[7]. Ibid. pp. 135-136.

[8]. Ibid. p. 158.

[9]. Ibid. p. 162.

[10]. Ibid. p. 165.

[11]. Ibid. p. 389.

[12]. Ibid. p. 436.

[13]. G.R. Coulthard, "The Situation of the Writer in Contemporary Cuba", CARIBBEAN STUDIES, Vol. 7, No. 1, 1967, p. 30.

[14]. L. King, "Mr. Black in Cuba" ASAWI Bulletin No. 5, Dec. 1972, p. 25.

[15]. Guillén, Obra poética 1958-1972, Vol. II, (La Habana, 1973), p. 108.

[16]. Keith Ellis, "Literary Americanism and the Recent Poetry of Nicolás Guillén.", UTQ, Vol. XLV, Number 1, Fall, 1975, pp. 1-18.

[17]. Guillén, Obra poética, Vol. II, op. cit. p. 375-376.

CHAPTER THREE

THE HISTORICAL FOCUS
"HIstory, Society & Change"

The work of Guillén reflects a variety of recurring concerns among which the historical evolution of the Cuban society takes pride of place. This preoccupation with the historical process by which Cuba has arrived at its present level of attainment is a part of a wider predilection for history among Latin American and Caribbean writers, especially since 1940. Men of Guillén's generation like Eduardo Mallea of Argentina (1902), Alejo Carpentier of Cuba (1904), or Enrique A. Laguerre of Puerto Rico (1906) and younger writers like Wilson Harris of Guyana (1921), E. Kamau Brathwaite of Barbados (1930), Carlos Fuentes of Mexico (1929). or Derek Walcott of St. Lucia (1930), among others, have constantly sought either to discover the "soul" of their country in its history, (its "intra-historia") or to develop a historical perspective that helps to define and explain the contemporary reality with all its dilemmas and challenges.

Carpentier, Mallea and Harris, in particular, speak of this deeper historical process that needs to be captured and given form in literature since it provides the real sediment of an evolutionary consciousness that is often not represented in the official, pseudo-scientific, historical records. While Harris talks of subtle links hidden beneath the surface which contradict or counterbalance the records of divisiveness and conflict, Mallea talks of the two faces of the national experience, the visible and the invisible faces of Argentina, and Carpentier insists that, inspite of the errors, absurdities and monstrosities recorded in the thirty centuries of Latin American history, it must be recognized that the region's *style*, its character, has to be defined in terms of its history.[1]

Much of this concern for history and historical perspectives is born out of a strictly nationalist and regionalist sentiment and bears testimony to conscious gropings towards the discovery of an authentic national identity and nationalist expression in art. As such then, it is part of a growing regional cocern that dates back to the early nineteenth century attempt by writers like Andrés Bello to find an "origial" view of history by which to evaluate and interpret the forces at work in the societies to which they felt committed. Bello's impassioned appeal to young writers, historians and intellectuals in 1848, in his "El Araucano", lays a foundation that is instructive:

> We would like to save it (treatment and study of the American experience) from an excessive servility to the science of civilized Europe... Learn to judge for yourselves: aspire to independence of thought. Drink from the fountains, at least from the streams close to those sources... Our civilization will also be judged by its works and if it is found to be copying European civilization slavishly even in what is not applicable to us, what will Michelet or Guizot (French historians) say of us? They will say: "America has not shaken off its chains: it is crawling in our footsteps blindfolded...[2]

The real burden of Bello's speech is for a recognition of the value of history and for an informed and critical evaluation of the historical process in its relation to the pursuit of national independence in all its forms - cultural, intellectual, political, social and economic.

Guillén's concern for history is inspired by this same principle which he outlined in his historic address to the First National Congress of Writers and Artists in August, 1961 which established the Union of Writers and Artists of Cuba (UNEAC) of which he was sole President until he died. Having reviewed the history of the independence struggle from the mid-nineteenth century onwards, he then posed the following question: "Now, then, while all this was going on, what has the stand of the intellectual been and what should it be in the context of the new state of things created by the Revolution? To answer that question, we must retrace the history of our motherland and return to the origins of our nation at the start of the last century".[3] And the express reason for this backward glance is to help shape a forward thrust in the building of "a culture that responds to our Revolutionary reality and our historical formation".[4] In an interview with Shiela Graham in Havana in 1975, Guillén reiterated this position by stressing that "each of our peoples is branded with the colonial mark... and one must examine them in relation to the *historical* context of each of these peoples: one dare not talk in abstract terms".[5]

THE AMNESIAC EXPERIENCE

There seem to be three distinct levels of response to history on Guillén's part, which can be summarized as: the amnesiac experience, the divisive encounter and the integrating perception. The first of these has to deal with the historical connection prior to the Negro diaspora or beyond the Middle Passage. The African connection for Guillén is, in essence, a mere emotion and a vague memory. "El apellido" is the tortured experience of a people who have lost their African identity but who find consolation in a newly discovered Cuban/Caribbean/Universal identity. Africa can only be recalled in dreams, visions and sensations, or through symbols - rhinoceros, baobab, lance, monkeys, snakes - or, as in "Balada de los dos abuelos", as

> Africa of humid jungles
> and enormous muffled gongs.[6]

His situation is reminiscent of Derek Walcott's, in "Laventille", where he seems to abhor the back-to-Africa trends of the sixties even after he has moaned in "A Far Cry From Africa": "How can I turn from Africa and live?" In "Laventille", Walcott turns around to ask:

> Which of us cares to walk
> even if God wished
> those retching waters where souls were fished'
> for this new world?[7]

because:

> Something inside is laid wide like a wound,
> some open passage that has cleft the brain,
> some deep amnesiac blow. We left
> somewhere a life never found,
> customs and gods that are not born again.[8]

This cleavage and dismemberment is seen by Guillén as the great tragedy of the Middle Passage in which the African identity was "seized" and deliberately forgotten by the captors, so that what is remembered of the Middle Passage itself is simply:

> Ships and more ships!
> Negroes and more Negroes![9]

What Guillén does not deny, is that there is at least a vague memory and a creative contribution in the cultural seeds brought across the waters by the ancestors who came in chains. These seeds have been sown in Cuban soil, have been fertilized and have helped to produce a national mould, so that there is really no longer any need to go back beyond the Middle Passage. Like Walcott in "the Swamp", he will not go:

> Backwards to darkness, go black
> With widening amnesia. . .[10]

Guillén entertains no notions of mythical links with Africa. He accepts the cruel but formal dismemberment caused by history.

In a way, this position is later adopted by the young Trinidadian poet Victor Questel, but without the anguish of Guillén's "El apellido" or the puzzlement of Walcott's "A Far Cry From Africa" and the grief of Choc Bay". Questel concludes:

> I have no grief
> for words to
> flounder upon
>
> for the way lost
> is the way
> lost.[11]

In this way, however, he differs significantly from Brathwaite who, without losing sight of his Caribbean moorings and identity, perceives meaningful connections in a "gut" link with the African matrix from which history attempted to dismember him. Brathwaite dares to recross the Middle Passage in *Masks*, chooses "to dare the ships" and go back to Africa in search of ancestral roots, by way of a symbolic return through time and space. The journey may not confirm all that was anticipated through dreams that had tried to span the miles and the years of exile

> to seas
> of bitter edges
>
> whips of white worlds
> stains of new
>
> rivers.[12]

but the encounter proves rewarding.

The returning son/exile/stranger, at the end of *Rights of Passage*, is asking questions about identity, heritage and dispossesion, in a way that seems similar to those of Guillén in "El apellido":

> Where then is the nigger's
> home? . . .
> Will exile never
> end? . . .
>
> The memories
> are cold: . . .
>
> What we
>
> can't touch
> will never
> be enough
> for us to shout
>
> about, who live
> with God -
>
> less rock
> the shock
>
> of dis-
> possession.[13]

But he rediscovers that other half of himself which the Middle Passage, time, history and exile had threatened with Walcott's "widening amnesia", with cold memories, ashes and smoke. Unlike Guillén he does not give up in despair, nor hope that from some *vague* country, *distant* cousins will emerge from some *remote* jungle with little snatches of his *remote* blood. Brathwaite's rediscovery of Africa is not only physical, but cultural and spiritual, and it deals with more than a mere recognition of African survivals and retentions. It recaptures ancestral connections, meanings and significances. There is a sense of continuity through a living and comprehensive memory that provides the basis for the Negro's spiritual strength.

Damian Grant stresses the centrality of this vibrant memory in Brathwaite's vision of the Caribbean experiences when he says:

> If his color is his physical identity, his memory is the Negro's spiritual identity: the short memory that takes him back to slavery . . . and the long memory that takes him back to beyond this. . . back to tribal wars. . . , back to drums and dancing, back to the reassurance of forests and rivers. . . .his memory is an active thing . . .[14]

He plants himself squarely in the bosom of the culture from which he had been snatched, not through romantic exultation, but as a concrete encounter with the other self; an encounter through which he experiences an "awakening", a sense of renewal and a revitalizing revelation that must now underpin a newly found confidence that equips him to come to terms with his Caribbean reality where his navel string is, in fact, buried.

On the question of the Caribbean experience, Guillén and Brathwaite came closer together: the one confident in his universal brotherhood of man and caught up in a universal proletarian struggle, but without any special reference to Africa, and the other confident in the fact that as an individual, he has redicovered the real value of Africa for the reintegration of the Caribbean personality and for a sense of wholeness. For both, the experience in the Caribbean is the central preoccupation: the impact of divisive forces, the struggle for survival and the shaping of a new identity and a destiny.

THE DIVISIVE ENCOUNTER

Guillén sees the history of the Caribbean from the Middle Passage onwards as the history of a society in formation, with all the tensions, contradictions, errors and achievements that such a process involves. In "Balada de los dos abuelos" he establishes a direct historical connection between the Middle Passage and the plantation:

> Ships and more ships!
> Negroes and more Negroes!
> What long splendor of cane!
> What a slave driver's whip!
> Stone of tears and of blood,

Half-open veins and eyes,
and empty mornings,
and plantation evenings,
and a great voice, a strong voice,
shattering the silence.
Ships and more ships,
what Negroes![15]

In "Elegía" he sees the arrival of the Europeans in terms of the arrival of greed, piracy, syphilis, whips, death, legal parchments and unfair rods:

Along the route of the sea
came the pirate,
harbinger of Evil Spirit. . .

One must learn to remember
what the clouds cannot forget. . .

Painful recollection to recall
what the clouds cannot forget
along the route of the sea.[16]

In "Sudor of látigo" he sees history in terms of oppression, exploitation and a picture of man's inhumanity to man, the kind of inhumanity that povokes reprisals and leaves the slave stained not only with the blood of the master he murders in his rage, but also with the blood that oozes out of his own wounded bare back. It is a history of dispossession under various paradoxical guises in "Mi patria es dulce por fuera":

My country is sweet on the outside
and very bitter on the inside. . .

I see blood and tears
beneath your light laughter. . .

The man from the interior
is sunken in a whole,
dead before he is born. . .

Today yankee, yesterday Spanish,

yes, Sir,
this land that is ours. . .[17]

In "Guadalupe W.I." it is a picture of a society whose history has created grave class problems and a scale of social and economic inequalities - the white Frenchmen enjoying a status of privilege and idleness; the Arabs dominating the commercial sector and the Negroes owning nothing, but producing everything as in "Caña":

The Negro
near the canefield.

The yankee
above the canefield.

The earth
beneath the canefield.

Our blood
being drained.[18]

The picture of the Caribbean that emerges in "West Indies Ltd." in many ways resembles the picture painted by the Puerto Rican Luis Palés Matos, for whom Caribbean history has been a negative, divisive and unprodutive experience. The dominant picture of West Indian society in his poetry is one of aridity, primitivism, pretentiousness, racial hatred and social and cultural underdevelopment. The history of the Caribbean has produced nothing of lasting quality, the Haitian Revolution produced only mimic men, Africa contributed only savagery and wild dreams and the U.S. introduced greed. For him, the Caribbean experience can be summed up in empty stereotypes - Haitian voodoo, Cuban santería and ñañaiguismo (Abakua cult), Jamaican rum and an incomprehensible dialect, unsuccessful imitation of Europe, French patois and calalou, the heat and papiamento of Curazao, the hurricanes of the Leeward and Windward Islands, tourism, obeah, sex, drumming and dancing. It is a picture of desolation, fragmentation, emptiness and vain dreams:

Antilles, my Antilles!
. . . all united,
dreaming, suffering and struggling
against pests, hurricanes and greed.[19]

And Guillén, to some extent, shares this view of the Caribbean as a prison where men are chained by economic circumstances, limited achievement and counter-productive rivalries. His poem, "Ancestros", crisply summarizes the spirit of recrimination and acrimony engendered by this divisive element in history:

> From what you say, Fabio,
> your grandfather was an archangel with his slaves.
> My grandfather, on the other hand,
> was a devil with his masters.
> Yours died from a stick lash.
> Mine, they hanged.[20]

The big difference between Palés Matos and Guillén, however, is that the former is trapped in that one-sided view of Caribbean history and society, whereas the latter sees another side to the coin.

THE INTEGRATING PERCEPTION

Guillén, like René Despestre, Edward Kamau Brathwaite and Wilson Harris, sees history as having a dynamic undercurrent of positive links and balances that deny the all-encompassing negativism of Palés Matos or of Vidia Naipaul of Trinidad. Despestre underlines the positive efforts at resistance and self-assertion on the part of the slaves first (on the West African coast by flight, on the slave ships by suicide, on the plantation by dissimulation and *cimarronaje*) and by the whole body of oppressed people who have refused to accept the imposed yokes and stereotypes and have progressively moved towards Revolution and change:

> It has been said that we, West Indians, represented
> the various stages of the same nightmare. . . one sees,
> not paradise-islands, but peoples frustrated by all
> sorts of socio-economic and socio-cultural aberrations
> . . . dominated by the coercive and violent force of
> under-development. . . (but) the Revolution, in fact, is
> breaking the emotional alienating circuits of the past,
> like those relating to racial dogma, and is creating
> in men reflections of fraternity and solidarity. . .
> this West Indian Revolution is ourselves, is our most
> authentic and profound identity, is a life-giving
> process of recovery of all the historical components
> of our personality.[21]

Brathwaite upholds the cultural continuum from ancestral Africa to the present which has fed and sustained the will and capacity for survival in the face of the most adverse social, political, economic and spiritual forces imposed by church, state and society. Harris defends the notion of getting "close to the inner universality of Caribbean man"[22] by way of exploring the "limbo-anancy syndrome" which illuminates the multifaceted experiences of Caribbean peoples in migration, and the imaginitive ways in which those migrants have transformed that disruptive and dismembering experience into an open and continuous gateway of constructive and creative possibilities. His way of doing this is to work towards "a philosophy of history which is original to us and yet capable of universal application",[23] one that involves an inner vision of wholeness, creativity and continuity against a visible background of fragmentation, sterilty, inferiority, waste and ruin.

Guillén's own positive vision has two dimensions - the belief that "the healing of the nations" is possible through an understanding of the dialectical process by which Caribbean history has evolved and the optimism that that understanding is inevitable as Caribbean peoples move into the Revolutionary phase of their history. The first aspect is amply illustrated in his treatment of the question of racial and cultural integration, in his vision of the proletarian identity of the yard folk-soldiers, policemen, peasants, workers, trade union leaders and artists who must collaborate to defeat inimical forces that convert history into a nightmare of division and dispossession, and in his conception of the Caribbean and Latin American destiny as being a common, united fight for full democracy, human dignity and unrestricted independence.

The second aspect is based on the principle that society is not static and that change is inevitable. Guillén does not accept the Derek Walcott birth-death paradox of "laventille" as a dead-end where

> . . . some grill of light
> clanged shut on us in bondage. . .
>
> and in its swaddling cerements we're still bound,[24]

particularly when it is supported by the chaotic, choking frustrating view of the future in "The Swamp" where the "wild saplings" which could well symbolize youth and promise

> . . . take the edge
> Of nothing to them slowly, merge

Limb, tongue and sinew into a knot
Like chaos, like the road
Ahead.[25]

Guillén recognizes the facts of the urban experience of chaos and underdevelopment. He knows the big-city drifters moving in urban back-waters with souls that do not know the spice of laughter, and who, if they do, come out with a kind of wry, mocking utterance from cancerous guts; men hardened by the weight of deprivation and hunger but who never fall permanently into ruts, mud puddles of stagnant pools. The rural men, too, may get stuck in a hole, but they come out in the spirit of "Llegada" or, like the men in "Canción de los hombres perdidos" to hurl themselves onto the city. There is no image of social paralysis for there is always a way out. The "paloma de veulo popular", the symbolic dove, the bearer of good news, is constantly hovering over his society with a message that inspires the indomitable will of the people to be free.

When Guillén personifies the sugar-cane in "West Indies Ltd." (Section 3) and they tremble, fear and sing, he is pointing to the collective will of the people who will rise up in revolt. Again, they wave their "hands" to the revolutionary way out of the sugar dilemma.

The idea of "the open future" recurs in poems such as "Elegía a un soldado vivo", "Casa de vecindad", and "Guitarra", as the symbol of the open possibilities for the fulfillment of the collective dreams and hopes of the people. In "El banderón" the poet pauses to look at the possibility of illusion or the vanity of dreaming, but this is already counteracted by the conviction that the collective energies of the people will triumph:

With my soul in living flesh,
I dream and I work below;
soon, the man below will be on top
when the one on top is below.
With my soul in living flesh,
I dream and I work, below.
("Cuando yo vine a este mundo")[26]

The destiny he is dealing with here is not a Cuban destiny. It is the destiny of the entire Caribbean, "Antillilandia", as he calls it in "Casa de vecindad", a region awaiting the trumpet call to Judgment, from which point it will be able to look back on history and say with Jesús Menéndez:

The journey was long and the road was rough.
A tree grew up with the blood from my wound.
A bird sings from it an ode to life.
Dawn is announced with a trill.[27]

NOTES

1. Wilson Harris, "History, Fable and Myth in the Caribbean and Guianas", CARIBBEAN QUARTERLY, Vol. 15. No.2, June 1970, pp. 1-32; Eduardo Mallea, Historia de una pasión argentina, (Buenos Aires, 1935); Alejo Carpentier, Tientos y diferencias, Mexico, 1964.

2. Andrés Bello, "El Araucano", quoted in Anderson Imbert - Florit, Literatura Hispano-americana, Tomo 1, 1970, p. 260.

3. Nicolás Guillén, Prosa de prisa, Tomo 11, La Habana, 1975, pp. 419-420.
4. Ibid. p. 429.

5. Sheila Graham, "Three Responses to the Caribbean Experience: Cesaire, Braithwaite and Guillén", (Essay presented as a Caribbean Study for the B.A. at U.W.I. (Mona), April, 1976), p. 3.

6. Guillén, Obra poética, Vol. I, p. 138.

7. Derek Walcott, The Castaway, London, 1965, p.34.

8. Ibid. p. 35.

9. Guillén, Obra poética, Vol. I, p. 138.

10. Walcott, op. cit. p. 12.

11. Victor D. Questel and Anson Gonzalez, Scorez, Trinidad, 1972.

12. Brathwaite, Masks, London, 1968. p. 70.

13. Brathwaite, Rights of Passage, London, 1967. pp. 78-79.

14. Damian Grant, "Emerging Image: The Poetry of Edward Brathwaite, CRITICAL QUARTERLY, Vol. 12. No. 2. Summer, 1970, p. 187.

15. Guillén, Obra poética, Vol. I., pp. 138-139.

16. Ibid. pp. 239-240.

[17]. Ibid. pp. 225-226.

[18]. Ibid. p. 129.

[19]. Luis Palés Matos, Poesía: 1915-1956 (Puerto Rico, 1957).
See Also: Poesía, CASA, La Habana, 1975, p. 83.

[20]. Guillén, Obra poética, Vol. II, p. 285.

[21]. René Depestre, "Problems of Identity for the Black Man in Caribbean Literatures", CARIBBEAN QUARTERLY , Vol. 19. No. 3. pp. 59-61.

[22]. Wilson Harris, op. cit. p. 7.

[23]. Ibid. p. 29.

[24]. Walcott, op. cit. p. 35.

[25]. Ibid. p. 12.

[26]. Guillén, Obra poética, Vol. I, p. 235.

[27]. Ibid., p. 436.

CHAPTER FOUR

THE SOCIAL THRUST

"Voices From The *Yard*"

One of the possible contradictions that can arise when writers or their critics are dealing with the experience of the dispossessed is illustrated in this criticism of Nicolás Guillén's treatment of the Negro in Cuba:

> ...it is easy to argue that Guillén's advocacy of multiracial solidarity, of a mullato culture, is not only wholesome but the result of caution, It is clear that for Guillén the black man in Cuba was mostly an exploited Cuban, discriminated against perhaps, but with no real problem of identity. His verse therefore shows no sensitivity to the notion that blacks in Cuba have lived in the context of a ghetto[1] or a minority culture. The stress and strain were seen as essentially economic...[2]

DEFINITIONS:

"Words are mysterious and that is important." These words, taken from a lecture given at the University of Guyana in March 1976 by Tony Hurley[3], are reminiscent of the Zohar with all its Cabalistic preoccupation with the deeper meanings and mysteries of language particularly in terms of the mystic beliefs of the Jews of the Diaspora. However, the quote takes on concrete significance when one is dealing with all-embracing and all-pervasive words such as literature, politics and culture which encompass concepts which are not infrequently deeply and intricately inter-related, particularly when dealing with the Africans of the other Diaspora.

It is often dangerous to regard poltiics only as the institutional framework which makes operational provisions for the ordering of people's social and economic activities. It can be equally dangerous to restrict culture to the notion of some amorphous admixture of "civilised" patterns of behaviour, "cultivated" artistic tastes and expression and recognisably disparate or homogenous folk traditions or to conceive of a ghetto culture as something separate from the ghetto economy. The problem of classification of experience is especially acute when one is dealing with the multifarious totality of the experience of people who have undergone the drama and trauma of enslavement, dislocation, dispossession, alienation, and exploitation, especially of the kind that has characterised the Caribbean experience of colonialism and imperialism.

Without getting trapped in the creation or imitation of clichés, one needs to acknowledge that the values, beliefs, habits, customs, strategies, aspirations and anxieties of the dispossessed peoples of the Caribbean in their struggle for survival have formed the basis of a composite life-style and has given rise to what some might call a culture of poverty[4] or variously: a culture of underdevelopment, a culture of survival, a culture of resistance or a culture of change. Such a situation automatically shatters any conceptual barriers which would seek to differentiate between culture and politics or between culture and the socio-economic conditions that are the reality lived and faced by those people who are supposed to be the possessors of that distinct culture.

Lloyd King quite appropriately recognises the reality "of a ghetto or minority culture" which would presume a full appreciation of the entire, composite context of that ghetto world. But when he argues that because of Guilléns's insistence on the primacy of the economic stress and strain, his verse *shows no sensitivity* to that culture, he is denying the very validity of the concept of a "ghetto culture" which would necessarily be based in the socio-economic realities of the ghetto.

We have argued elsewhere[5] that Guillén's advocacy of multiracial solidarity and the national mulatto experience is an idealistic, humanistic position guided by an intuitive response to national realities and nationalist goals, rather than a scientific or pseudo-scientific conclusion about the anthropology of the Negro and his neighbours or co-partners in the Cuban experience. It is rather less than true to say that for Guillén the Negro has "no real problem of identity". What is nearer the truth is that his real problem of identity has to be seen not merely in racial terms but in the context of the full realities of his *culture of underdevelopment* or his *culture of survival.*

This is the major thrust of what one might call the "*yard*" poetry of Guillén. The "solar", "casa de vecindad" and "accesoria"[6] have been variously used by him as focal points for the treatment of socio-economic and political issues at the national level, no doubt because they represent a microcosmic crystallisation of a range of experiences that would otherwise be described diversely as social, cultural, economic and political. In the barrack-*yard* or baracoon they are simply the sediment of a culture which defines itself in human struggle for survival.

The simple act of turning to the "*yard*" is not, in itself, an unusual phenomenon since Spanish Caribbean writers[7] have repeatedly used the "barracón", "barriada", "barrio" and "batey" in the same way that Latin American writers have often looked to the "favela", "barrio" and "arrabal" as *causa máxima* for protest writing. Guillén's real claim to special consideration rests in the poetic texture of his treatment of the themes of dispossession and "*yard* culture" and the particular angle of vision he adopts in developing a progressively revolutionary understanding of the "*yard*" situation and its con-comitant challenges. "Words never fall into a vacuum" says the Zohar[8], and Guillén's poetry from *Motivos de son* (1930) up to *La rueda dentada* falls into a readily discernible line that links selected poems such as "Hay que tené voluntá", "Llegada", "Sabás", "Balada de Símon Caraballo", "No sé por qué piensas tú", "Visita a un solar", "Casa de vecindad", "Coplas de Juan Descalzo", "El hambre", and "Problemas del subdesarrollo" in an on-going concern with the role of the dispossessed in the transformation of society not only on the local or national scene but at the regional and international levels as well.

YARD POETRY

The main concern of this chapter is to show how important a role the *yard* has played in the evolution of Guillén's poetry and to show the extent to which the products come to characterise Guillén's method and outlook. The study starts with his early radical and "revolutionary" approach to the Negro's condition in Cuba and leads into the ideological Revolutionary stand that has earned him the title of National Poet of Revolutionary Cuba.

His first major evolutionary effort in poetry was born in the *yard* context of Havana but only after he had explored other forms and styles. Prior to his *Motivos de son*, Guillén concerned himself primarily with themes and a style that betrayed no real revolutionary instinct or inclination. Stylistically, he was caught up in the imitative exercises of young poets who sought to emulate the Modernistic experiments of Rubén Darío without being able to capture the finesse and daring successes of their master. Angel Augier's comment on *Cerebro y corazón* (1922), Guillén's first collection of poems from his adolescent days, is very instructive on this score: "This book shares the virtues and defects of Cuban poetry in the first three lustra of this century when the all-powerful influence of Rubén Darío and his followers was predominant - *Modernismo* in its declining days, now reduced to overused images, pedantic turns of phrase and commonplace formulae."[9] But another comment by Augier about Guillén's first serious exposure to literary circles in Havana as a youngster bordering on adulthood is equally instructive, because it reveals an anxiety to find new forms of expression that would mark a definitive break with *Modernismo*: "He attended the iconoclastic *tertulias* of the café *Martí* where the members of that youthful pleiad helped to twist the neck of Rubén Darío's swan."[10] It was at this stage, too, that Guillén seemed to have come into a phase of strong disillusionment with University and society sharing, with other young writers, what Augier calls "militant non-conformity with the surrounding cultural mediocrity." This is the period of his sonnets, "Al margen de mis libros de estudio" (1922), which mark the beginning of a short crisis period of personal revolt and unproductivity and the first marginal signs of an uneasy spirit being inclined towards protest.

It is out of that phase of revolt and silence that the poet emerged with his revolutionary *yard* poetry in *Motivos de son*, a novel poetic expression that was instinctively and implicitly "revolutionary", in content, form and style. Even if the mere inclusion of Negro themes did not seem distinctively innovative since other Cubans, particularly white "negrista" writers, were already imitating the Africanist fad of European artists of the time, Guillén carved out a unique path for himself by using this as an opportunity to look seriously at the harsh realities of the ghetto, the particularities of its culture and its contribution to a proper definition of a national cultural heritage. Even to that extent, he was unusually adventurous and "revolutionary"; but to find a medium through which to convey the *yard* themes or *motivos* he had to go into the soul of the *yard* and draw on their folkways, their speech patterns and rhythms, their music and dance, the cultural sediment that could "twist the music out of hunger".[11] "For that he needed the *son*."

The adoption of the *son* as a poetic medium was a bold and "revolutionary" act that, for the first time, was validating for the middle and upper classes, and particularly the sophisticated circles of the literary elite, a vital creative form which had emerged from among the Negro communities of Oriente Province. It had now found its way to their Havana counterparts in the ghettoes of the capital and subsequently the salons of the upper classes.

In a way, Guillén was performing this "revolutionary" act unconsciously at first, more by inspiration and impulse than by calculation or design. He himself confesses that the first poem "Negro bembón" came to him from the repeated sound of two words *negro bembón* which he heard in his sleep.[12] His first response was to get out of bed and write the poem which had assailed his sub-conscious. He wrote that and about ten others which he published as *Motivos de son*.[13] The event was all the more "revolutionary" because of the burning prejudices that existed in Cuban high society and in literary circles against the society and culture of the ghetto- their dialect forms, the so-called "immorality" of their *rumba*, *son* and *bongó*, their rum and dance and their social relationships, attitude and values. The comments of Ramón Vasconcelos on *Motivos de son* are indicative of some attitudes of the time:

> Guillén...should not be shaking hands with any gadabout, easy, vulgar and dislocated street muse ... The *son* does not need to be a medium of social protest... (Guillén) ought to universalise his verse and ideas instead of locating them in the *yard* (*solar*) where thay can dance to the sound of the bongo drum.[14]

Although Vasconcelos tries to excuse his stand by saying that he does not detest the use of the vernacular and that the *son* has its place and should be allowed to retain its true character, the crucial consideration here is that he opposes Guillén's spiritual association with that popular character whom he calls "the anonymous bard in the idle and care-free setting of the *yard* (accesoria)".

Guillén's real possible *faux pas* was to fall victim to that kind of criticism and allow himself to become self-conscious to the point of surrendering a vital part of the cultural matrix that subsisted in that *yard* culture - the popular idiom - in the name of universality. His *coup de maitre* nevertheless was his adherence to the *son* form.

Another critic writing in 1930, Regino E. Boti, described Guillén's poems as "gold dust" precisely because the artist's ear was attuned to all the vital sources and "lyrical palpitations of that sector of the Cuban populace that was least understood."[15] What Boti was emphasising was the richness of the elemental rhythms from which Guillén could draw to strengthen his blend of metric, musical and popular rhythms in poetry.

YARD CULTURE

Whatever the successes of Guillén have been one cannot but observe that the abandoning of the vernacular, the folk idiom, must have considerably restricted the potential of his later poetry to fathom the soul of the folk culture of the *yard*, particularly after *Sóngoro Cosongo* (1931). The *son* was never intended for formal Spanish diction or metrics. The cradle and natural habitat of the *son* was the popular idiom, in the same way that the calypso and West Indian creoles are inextricably linked. This does not mean, necessarily, that rich poetic effects cannot be achieved by the adoption of the musical rhythm of the *son* or calypso to speech patterns that would seem to approximate to formal or standard Spanish or English.

What Gordon Rohlehr says of Edward Braithwaite's poem, "Calypso", can also be said of many of Guillén's *son*-poems. Rohlehr speaks of the "metric organisation of speech rhythm to suggest the syncopation of music" and the conviction that the calypso in general "provides us with living examples of a very complex *metric* organisation of language". For Rohlehr, the creative exercise involves more than the mere, token use of speech rhythms and idioms. It means "being conscious of the syncopated drum rhythms in the background" and being able "to blend words with extremely complex rhythmic phrases of music and still retain the fluidity and basic rhythms of speech". But it also takes into account the essential part that popular West Indian speech has to play in the calypso-poem and in the creole-poem. Sparrow's musical language in his calypso-poems, A.J. Seymour's poem "To a Calypsonian", Braithwaite's "Calypso", Walcott's experiment in Chapter VI of "Tales of the Islands", Malik's "Pan Run II" and numerous other creations grounded in popular speech and related rhythms are now regarded as artistic expressions of comparable value.[16]

What this says to the West Indian reader of Guillén is that the contribution of the *yard* folk to the enrichment of the national mulatto culture must have been somewhat circumscribed if not impaired by the abandonment of the genuine folk idiom of the *yard.* This becomes even more pronounced when one recognises that Guillén repeatedly chooses to use the speaking voice of "the people" in preference to the distant or objective voice of the poet-observer; but it is a speaking voice without the particularities of that folk idiom. Indirectly, however, this change to a formal idiom serves to highlight the real value of that initial folk outburst from the ghetto in *Motivos de son.*

The burden of that collection of poems is not argued; it is dramatised, and its content is simply this: that the real texture of life in the *yard* can effectively be captured in the idiom and rhythms of the *yard* culture; that the message of protest does not need to be clothed in vituperation since the reality of that culture has a forcefulness and vigour of its own; and that the elements of that culture - music, dance, privation, hunger, love, desertion, struggle, protest, persecution and related values and attitudes - have a cohesiveness that manifests itself in a concerted and energetic demand for change.

The actual physical setting and characters of the *Motivos de son* are undoubtedly similar to the *yard* settings of Roger Mais' *The Hills Were Joyful Together* or Orlando Patterson's *The Children of Sysiphus* or perhaps even Douglas Archibald's *The Rose Slip* - a small *yard* community shut in upon itself with all its problems and creating a sense of kinship in distress. It is a little enclave of poverty that produces its own strategies for survival out of fear of self-destruction. The harsh realities of underdevelopment are there - unemployment, pimping, prostitution, the vain cry for money for the bare essentials of life, problems of male irresponsibility and indications of female ingenuity. The attendant tensions, petty conflicts and frustrations of that closed and stifling world come to the surface in the form of racial hang-ups, quarrels over claims of ugliness and beauty, colour prejudice, in-fighting among blacks of varying shades and petty jealousies and anxieties on the part of deserted lovers who cannot maintain their women.

CULTURE OF SURVIVAL

The conditions of this world inevitably breed their own morality, a morality of survival: any means to an end; no love without money, at least, for food; flirt with the tourist and pander to his whims and fancies; entertain no scruples about deserting an impoverished lover; opt for prostitution even if people frown. It is a matter of a psychology of survival that surely pays due respect to notions of fidelity and love, but which bows in the face of disaster in order to survive and fight another day. In fact, the element of hope stands out clearly in "Hay que tené voluntá" where a voice similar to that of Bob Marley's[17] in "No woman no cry" sings out:

Mus' have will power
'cause bad luck
ain''t goin las' forever!
Go on, darlin an' don't cry
Go dat way:
Go, an' don't cry, sugar
Come dis way;
Go on, darlin', go on,
Mus' have will-power!

The voices that are heard emanating from the *yard* alongside that hopeful strain bear a variety of tones and challenges which are unmistakably born out of the ethos and culture of the *yard.* There is the kind of music that is not overtly tinged with any note of protest, as in the poems, "Quirino", "Madrigal", "Mujer nueva", "Secuestro de la mujer de Antonio", "Rumba" and "Velorio de Papá Montero". What exudes from this body-corporate of the *yard* is a life-style characterised by dance and song, sensuality and rum, the guitar and maracas, the *tres* and *son*, daggers and occasional murders, wakes and mourning and days and nights of rejoicing and festivity. Guillén himself speaks of Papá Montero, the *son* specialist as "son of the fete, of rum and music, whose throne is firmly established in the heavens of (Cuban) folkore".[18] But these are all products of the *yard* - Quirino operationg from the warmth of his *accesoria* and Papá Montero and the rumba dancers coming straight from the *solar*. What one gets is an inside view of their ways of coping with the stark realities of the *yard.* They can drown their miseries in the ecstacy of song, dance, laughter, sex and rum, or shroud their frustrations in outbursts of violence against their own close friends ("ecobios"). In a way, the situation does look somewhat like that of Walcott's "Laventille" where "we dare a laugh,

> ritual, desperate words,
> born like these children from habitual wombs,
> from lives fixed in the unalterable groove
> of grinding poverty.[19]

The real difference, however, lies in the fact that the people in Guillén's *yard* refuse to remain trapped in the "swaddling cerements" that held Laventille bound in "habitual wombs"/tombs, content merely to gaze across the void upon a world of privilege that is "beyond" them; neither are they merely "invisible, faceless and voiceless" poor people

> "Dulled by their galvanized dungeons
> In the step-steepled Laventille
> And the Caroni of their sorrows."

They do not just occasionaly "erupt into violence and visibility".[20] They have a voice, and the tone of that voice is not one of merriment. The image of the flamboyant, "happy-go-lucky", underdog with a "calypso mentality" disappears to give way to a serious, meditative, critical voice of protest which eventually develops into a "voice which is like a brutal thunder-peal in the throat".[21]

The type of *yard* character one sees in "Organillo" pumping his hurdy-gurdy without being able to get any continuous music from it and without any money in his pocket, though weak in himself, nevertheless finds moral support among the "arrivants" of "Llegada", who have invaded the city to swell the ranks of the dispossessed. This poem is rich with possible interpretations: the arrival of the Negro at the centre of literary expression, bringing with him all the untrapped resources piled up while he was relegated to the periphery of national literature; the emergence of a new literature that moves away from *Modernismo*, *vanguardismo*, *negrismo*, *et al* and brings a fresh dimension from the folk; the cultural and spiritual invasion of the city by creative rural folk who bring with them the vitality and vigour of their *son*; the invasion by the masses of the domains of privilege occupied by the rich; the awakening of the underdog to a level of consciousness that constitutes a new vision, a new focus, a new attitude to society and social change, a new presence and a new voice that sounds a clear prophetic and apocalyptic note.

VOICE FOR CHANGE

After "Llegada" the voice from the *yard* is firmer, more positive and aggresive. The "arrivants" have brought with them, not only the freshness of the fumes and vapours of the morning, but fire, knife, bow, fist, hard broad feet, and sweaty skins that reflect the tear-stained faces of the oppressed". They can understand the language of Braithwaite's Rastaman in "Wings of a Dove", who assumes the role of

> prophet and singer, scourge
> of the gutter, guardian
> Trench Town, the Dungle and Young's
> Town,...[22]

and who is sensitive to the agonies of, and outcry from, the *yard* situation.

Yard music after "Llegada" then assumes new proportions. The very musical instruments of protest: "La canción del bongó" attacks racial prejudice in profound satirical tones, "Maracas" attacks subservience to U.S. imperialism and their tourist culture, and "Guitarra" comes with its mixture of laughter and tears to capture the sighs of the people and their dreams for the future. It is the popular troubadour José Ramón Cantaliso who takes hold of that "mature guitar" which is pregnant with *sones* about the anguish of the *yard* folk, and emerges from the *solar* with his

> voice of cancerous guts
> fume of the *solar* and sugar cane.

He and Juan Cocinero sing about their *yard* neigbours Juana, Carlos, Luis, Pedro, Norberto, Petra and their problems of cramped housing, unemployment, tuberculosis, rent and eviction. They are dealing with issues that express the anguish and concerns of other *yard* characters such as Simón Caraballo, Luis the candy vendor, Juan el Barbero, Juan Bimba, Juan Descalzo, Juan Sin Nada, Juan Pueblo among others.

It is this plethora of voices from the *yard* that constitutes the early radical element in Guillén's poetry. The socially ostracised Negro who hitherto had no real voice in literature now comes to the heart of literature, not as a literary curiosity or a symbol of primitivism and sensuality , but essentially as a human voice with deep human concerns and an important social outlook. Musical instruments and musical forms that have heretofore been despised in the cultivated and "civilised" circles of the elite are taken from the *yard* and given a dominant role to play in communicating a new radical message to those conservative quarters. Guillén himself explains the specific role of the bongo drum in his "Canción del bongó". "It is a satirical poem whose elements are well known in Cuba since they are born out of racial conflict, our mulatto experience. It is the bongó drum which presides over our quarrell, which knows our origin and speaks finally with the serious voice of a grandfather, tearing away once and for all the curtain which can hardly hide our past".[23] One can understand why the poet calls upon his popular guitarrist to wipe the alcohol from the mouth of his guitar when one considers that the *son* form and its bongo, maracas and popular guitar were generally regarded as immoral and socially unacceptable because of their central role in *yard* culture. It is a symbolic act of purification, the wiping away of social stigmas and the clearing of the way for a message of social renewal.

To achieve this, Guillén makes his *yard* characters look in on themselves with a critical eye at the same time that they look out on the wider society with an eye towards reform. The *yard*, for Guillén, is a commune of sufferers, a breeding ground of protest and solidarity among the dispossessed. Through the *yard* and its characters he can explore the different faces of hunger, different levels of awareness and protest and the range of deep human concerns to which a committed poet and Revolutionary activist must address himself.

There is an implied comment on traditional views about activities such as prostitution, in the poet's refusal to engage in any puritannical moralising over the decisions and actions of his characters. He places such social "evils" in their true socio-economic perspective, recognising them as the outgrowth of a whole system that could produce the *yard* communities and tax the ingenuity of the "sufferers" to find means of survival. He sees the black woman from the *yard* not primarily as a sex symbol nor merely as a rumba dancer as other poets of his time did, but more as central figure in the *yard* commune - a source of pride to the self-conscious and half-insecure black man, as a bread-earner in the *yard* family and as the dominant personality who rouses the lazy dandy from his illness and complacency and sends him out to find work.

More than being just a mere commune of sufferers and a breeding ground of protest, the *yard* becomes a crucible for the moulding of popular solidarity and a centre for rehabilitation and reintegration of the personality. His soldiers, for example, in his *Cantos para soldados...* are being persuaded to acknowledge their affinity to the *yard* community. The voice of the persona who pleads with the misguided soldier in "Soldado aprende a tirar" or in "No sé por qué piensas tú" is not just the poet Guillén. It is a voice from the *yard* that recognises the diverse role of external forces that seek to split the *yard* community (symbolic now of the entire proleteriat) and destroy all potential for solidarity and resistance. That voice from the "dry room" in "Riesgo y ventura de dos soldados" also sounds like another voice from the solar that invites the soldiers not simply to find physical warmth and rest but to find a new experience of rehabilitation among their own people; hence the warm reception and almost ritual celebration on their return. His experience is like that of Pedro Cortés in "Soldado libre" who returns to his peasant family to find rehabilitation in singing, laughing, dancing and the joy of rearing children, kissing their foreheads and tasting peace and freedom.

The concept of the reintegrated *yard* community therefore amplifies the poet's Revolutionary vision and strengthens the hope for social reform through popular solidarity and militancy. The "strong fist" of the "arrivants" in "Llegada" strengthens the "closed fist" of protest artists like the Negro Simón Caraballo, and joins with the "titanic and avenging fists" of the workers in "West Indies Ltd.", so that the struggle and the consciousness that start in the *yard* now embrace the national working class, particularly after the national crises of the 1933-37 period. The urban beggar, Sabás, from the *yard* community, will now close his open hand into a clenched fist to demand what is due him. Simón Caraballo will be imprisoned and executed for his protest songs, but the soldiers in "Diana" will take up his cause when the reveille finally sounds its Revolutionary note. And, indeed, the military experience, discipline and ballistic skill of the rural soldiers like Miguel Paz and his sergeant friend, are deemed to be crucial to the ongoing struggle.

CARIBBEAN VOICES

The Revolutionary tenor of Guillen's poetry in relation to the entire Caribbean and Latin American region is one that is clearly expressed in the image of the *yard*, an extension of the Cuban *yard*. The continental perspective is enunciated in his "Elegía a un soldado vivo" where the Cuban pariah identifies with his counterparts in Bolivia, Guatemala, Brazil and Haiti or in "Son venezolano" where the Cuban protest singer, Juan Bimba, identifies the bitter taste of the Cuban sugar experience in the Venezuelan petroleum experience, or where in "Barlovento" the hungry Cuban Negro finds his equal among the hungry, dispossessed, tuberculosis victims of Venezuelan black communities, or among the big-bellied children and hungry mendicant Negroes in the oil ports of Colombia. ("Una canción en el Magdalena"). The Caribbean perspective with the threat of domination by external forces is articulated very early in "West Indies Ltd.", but is given definitive *yard* identity much later as "Antillilandia" the "Casa de vecindad":

> Tenement-*yard*, back-*yard* of the Caribbean Sea,
> Where tenants meet
> beneath the moon, to talk;
> where there are Negroes still asking questions
> and women who killed their butterflies.
> Black-vermilion wave
> of workers with a bitter brow
> and children with aged faces,
> wounded by the fixed eye of the police.
> Land where blood sullies day...

and what is said is not written...[24]

The connections and references are clear: the region is seen as a kind of back-water, back-*yard*, exploited barrack-*yard* or underdeveloped tenement-*yard* by those who wish to continue to exploit its human and natural resources while despising their identifiable and valid culture and their potential for self-development. (See "Problemas del subdesarrollo").

The redeeming feature of this *yard* experience is captured in the symbolic use of the guitar and *son* to interpret not only the echoes of protest but the resonant notes of hope which the poet entertains:

A song of unleashed dream,
a simple song of death and life
with which to greet the bloody future,
red like the sheets, like the thighs, like the bed
of a woman newly delivered.[25]

And to reinforce that picture of a scathing *yard*, Guillén makes this comment to mark his historic visit to the University of the West Indies in 1974: "For what is irreversibly true is that the Caribbean is bubbling now more than ever like a cauldron of prophecies about to come true; an epic awakening... the people of the West Indies have lived in ignorance of one another, kept apart by the evil imperialist faith that divided them, that confronted them, face to face, like quiet ghosts. Mr. Haiti, Mrs. Jamaica, the Misses Guadeloupe and Martinique, Mr. Barbados, Mrs. Cuba...What can they say to one another in their English, in their patois, in their French, in their Spanish or in their papiamento? They have said little or nothing up to now, but right now they are begining to say more."[26] This is the beginning of a return to the fellowship of the *yard* and, consequently, the return to an experience of rehabilitation and integration of the Caribbean personality.

NOTES

[1] The tenement-*yard* or barrack-*yard* is characterized by over-crowded urban squatting and sub-standard housing at low-income rates of the kind commonly known in shanty-towns, "dungles," slums or ghettos, but strongly reminiscent of the barracoon inherited from slavery. West Indian writers like Roger Mais, C.L.R. James, Orlando Patterson, Austin Clarke, Douglas Archibald, Alfred Mendes, Alvin Bennett, Errol John, Roy A. Heath, Mervyn Morris, Dennis Scott, E.K. Brathwaite, Derek Walcott, Marguerite Wyke, Martin Carter and Abdul Malik have, from time to time, and in different ways, addressed themselves to the subject. James, Mendes and Guillén were writing on the subject in the 1930s.

[2] L. King, *ASAWI Bulletin*, No. 5, Dec. 1972, p. 25.

[3] Lecturer in the Dept. of French and Spanish Literature at the St. Augustine campus of the University of the West Indies. The theme: "Towards a Definition of French West Indian Literature."

[4] Oscar Lewis, Edmundo Desnoes, René Depestre have been singularly articulate on the themes of poverty, underdevelopment and resistance or survival respectively.

[5] See Chapter 6 and sub-title, "Identity, Race & Culture."

[6] "Solar" is the Cuban version of a tenement-house for poor working class families many of whom are unemployed.
"Casa de vecindad" falls more in the line of the barrack-*yard* or tenement-*yard* a small community of the lower classes sharing common premises.
"Accesoria" is a small room or hut usually occupied by servants in bourgeois residential areas. It was usually built near or even attached to the main houses like an annexe for purposes of obtaining light, water etc. This inevitably led to a community of working class people in the midst of the bourgeois community.

[7] Anselmo Suárez y Romero in 19th century Cuba; René Marqués and José Luis González in contemporary Puerto Rico; Manuel Zapata Olivella in the Negro communities of Colombia.

[8] Used as the opening epigraph in Ajejo Carpenter's *El siglo de las luces.*

[9] Angel Augier in Nicolás Guillén's *Obra Poética: 1920-1958* - Vol. I __________ "Prólogo," p. xviii.

[10] Ibid. p. xix.

[11] Edward Kamau Brathwaite, "The Twist" from *Rights of Passage*, op. cit., p. 40.

[12] Nicolás Guillén, *Prosa de prisa*: Tomo I, (La Habana, 1975), p. 294.

[13] Later editions have been stripped down to eight poems. "Curujey," "Me bendo caro" and "Ayé me dijeron negro" have been omitted.

[14] Ramón Vasconcelos, "Motivos de son," *Recopilación de textos sobre Nicolás Guillén*, op. cit., pp. 243-245.

[15] Regino E. Boti, "El verdadero son," ibid., p. 247.

[16] "Gordon Rohlehr's '*Sparrow and the Language of Calypso*' CAM Comment" - an interview between Edward Brathwaite and Gordon Rohlehr, CARIBBEAN QUARTERLY, Vol. 14. Nos. 1 & 2, pp. 91-96.

[17] Jamaica's leading reggae artist.

[18] Nicolás Guillén, *Prosa de prisa.* Vol. I, op. cit. p. 43.

[19] Derek Walcott, *The Castaway*, (London, 1965), p. 34.

[20] Gordon Rohlehr, "My Strangled City: Poetry in Trinidad 1964-75," CALIBAN Vol. II, #1 (Fall-Winter 1976); pp. 50-122.

[21] Guillén, *Obra Poetica (Vol. I)*, op. cit. p. 167.

[22] Brathwaite, *Rights of Passage*, op. cit., pp. 41-42.

[23] Guillén, *Prosa de prisa*, Vol, op. cit., p. 38.

[24] Nicolás Guillén, *Obra Poetica*, Vol. II, op. cit., pp. 18-19.

[25] Ibid. p. 19.

[26] See J.A. George Irish, "Notes on a Historic Visit: Nicolás Guillén in Jamaica," *CARIBBEAN QUARTERLY*, Vol. 21. Nos 1 & 2, March - June, 1975, p. 79.

CHAPTER FIVE

THE REVOLUTIONARY FOCUS OF HIS JOURNALISM

Nicolás Guillén is a writer whose zest for his profession and zeal for human progress are combined with three basic streaks in his personality - genuine altruism, sharp-witted rationality and sustained militancy. The overriding interest and the burning passion of his selected prose is revolutionary struggle in the service of humanity. This expresses itself in his ardent fervor against Fascism and its related atrocities of racism, dictatorship and philistinism on the one hand, and on the other, capitalism and its inevitable corollary, imperialism.

REVOLUTIONARY PENSADOR

Guillén is forever intensely involved in the task of observing, recording, internalizing and interpreting the events, scenes and people he encounters and, in the process, has developed an approach to journalism that rises above the mere reporting of melodramatic and sensational scenes and incidents. He is a revolutionary thinker and a serious analyst, a committed "pensador" within the Latin American tradition - a lover of liberal ideas and principles who is out in search of truth, justice, human understanding and human progress.He never evades a candid argument on matters of public interest. He works like an adult-educator whose main motivation seems always to be to have some message to transmit to his people without ever appearing to be a pedagogue.

This tendency comes out strongly in his interviews in Spain and on his trips through South America.[1] He is constantly trying to perceive connections and parallels, trying to deduce lessons and guidelines which would enhance the level of political and cultural awareness not only in Cuba, but in the entire Caribbean and Latin American region. His interview with the difficult and reticent Lieutenant - Colonel Modesto Guilloto during the Spanish Civil War has a dramatic and anecdotic quality which illustrates the calibre of the journalist with whom we are dealing - competent, determined, persistent, perceptive and persuasive:

> Now, from that moment, I decided to besiege him, cut short his retreat, in order to get to talk to him by any means. At the end of the function, I positioned myself on the stairway so that my prospective victim could not escape. And right there I accosted him as he came down. . .
> - Well, I have come to see you, because, as you well remember, I want to talk with you to get your impressions of the war and some news about your own life, so that people in Cuba and America might know about you.
>
> - Listen . . . I do not like these things. I believe that our task here and now is to fight; there is no time for photographs and interviews. All the action is on the front over there where there are fascists.
>
> - I think you are right, but only in part, Modesto. It is true that there is a lot to be done and that this is not the time to go around posing for the cinema. Nevertheless, I am sure it is your duty to speak to the people, not only the people of Spain who already know you and love you, but also the peoples of America who love you even without knowing you. All the masses of the Americas are supporting Spanish democracy, supporting the Republic, and

> any mention of your fighters stirs deepest
> sympathy and affection. How can you
> refuse to fight in this way for those
> very ideals that you defend with arms?
> That seems to me. . .

Modesto remains silent for a moment and finally accedes. . .[2]

In the spirit of that tradition of thinkers who move ahead of their societies and map out a liberal path for the development of their societies, Guillén places his poetry and prose at the service of his people directing their attention towards democracy and revolution. It is in this spirit that he rejects racism, and courageously opposes fascist dictatorships and chooses to assess the Cuban situation in Revolutionary terms, -identifying the historical and socio-economic forces that determine both the conditions of his people's existence and the nature of these relationships in that society. It is this analysis and understanding of the real conditions of life in his society, in the region and in the wider world, that constantly feeds a genuine altruism and supports his Revolutionary stance.

REVOLUTIONARY ALTRUISM

Intense human sympathy and understanding for suffering humanity and admiration for generosity and heroism are complementary and parallel currents in Guillén's prose, as in his poetry. He is acutely sensitive to situations in which people are placed at a disadvantage and manipulated in the interest of others. Not infrequently, these are circumstances that others are likely to take for granted, but they move the poet-journalist to respond profoundly to an underlying human anguish or struggle. At the same time, he always recognizes the positive dimensions of each traumatic experience and the possibilities for Revolutionary consciousness and action.

His account of an encounter with a child in Spain during the Civil War combines this sympathy and admiration in a way that eliminates any trace of pity or condescending patronage:

> I cannot forget those days when in one
> of those little towns found along the
> dramatic Spanish roads, I met a child
> who impressed me profoundly. He was half-
> naked, dressed only in short pants, and
> only about ten years old. When I saw him
> I approached him with the intention of

> trying to decipher something like a tatoo etched into his slender, brown arms. On one arm, in fact, I read, written in ordinary ink: "Death to the Fascists"; on the other there was the inscription: "They will not pass". I spoke with the child and learned that he was from Madrid where he always lived until he was forced to flee because of air raids. I learned that he had lost two brothers, children like himself, slain by bombers while playing at home. He was left with his mother alone, as his father had been killed on the battle-front. As I shook his hand, which he stretched out seriously, to say goodbye, he added: "Here, we are all poor; no one here has a thousand pesetas; we all work, and for the Franco forces to win, they will have to kill all of us!!"[3]

Similarly when he reviews the economic situation of the Haitian labourer in Cuba it becomes the starting point for a simultaneous review of the attributes and achievements of the Haitian people as a whole. He is sensitive to the language barrier and its related frustrations, the racial prejudice against the Haitian Negro, the modern versions of exploited Haitian slave labour on the Cuban sugar plantations, and popular prejudices against the poor migrant workers who invade Oriente Province and Camagüey. But against that picture he has clear ideas of the Haitian people as being "simple, kind, frugal, intelligent and clean" and, above all, "courageous in struggle in spite of an absence of material and spiritual help from outside".[4]

His contact with the Colombian oil-field workers of Barranca is the occasion for a touching exchange of ideas and sentiments between a poet-intellectual and a simple field hand, both of whom share a love for the creative and a deep sense of nationalism:

> "It is the first time that a poet or writer is coming here," that man whose skin was burnished by the sun told me. "They never come, neither the foreign ones nor the native ones. As far as the intellectuals are concerned, we do not exist; and the

> same applies to the owners of this enter-
> prise. Nevertheless, we enjoy poetry and
> books and we want to learn. Another thing:
> If you go back to Cuba, say that although
> we work out here, we are, first of all,
> Colombians. You already know the rest. . ."[5]

Guillén's response to this little speech is one of deep emotion: sadness tempered with hope, rather than despair. His new mission is to encourage more writers to leave their comforts and go out to communicate with the working man whose sensitivity is never dulled by hard manual labour.

This is an unquestionable call for revolutionary identification rather than mere patronage. His basic criterion for heroism is unselfish service and sacrifice in the interests of the proletariat. He sees José Martí, Antonio Maceo and Máximo Gómez as paradigms whose intellectual and military prowess was placed at the service of the masses with a sense of dedication and unselfishness that made personal sacrifice a matter of duty rather than a favour. Ignacio Agramonte in the 1860s and 70s, like Juan Marinello in the 1930s and 40s are men who left their aristocratic social circles, shed all the trappings of vain intellectualism and refinement to don the garb of the working class in struggle. As he says of Marinello, "by virtue of a process of self-sublimation, he was able to rise to the level of the people and begin a face dialogue with the man in the street".[6]

This preoccupation with the interests and destiny of the working class is not just a literary fad for Guillén. It is an altruistic involvement in a desperate struggle in self defense, and for self-determination. It is a political and economic struggle against exploitation and its off-shoots; a universal human struggle which transcends territorial and racial barriers without losing its immediacy of focus and purpose in each locale:

> This is one simple truth which must be
> driven home to the spirit of our people:
> over and above any red, yellow, black or
> white colour, there looms the terrible
> fact of material inequality, that monstrous
> distribution of the world's goods, and
> it is necessary to fight for a more just
> and equitable distribution. Where?
> Everywhere. In China, against Japan and
> those Chinese who turn their backs on
> their own people; in Venzuela, against
> governments that allow the English and

> Germans to suck out all of the oil from its soil rapaciously; in the West Indies, against the greed of the sugar, banana and mining interests of the United States; in Spain, against Italy and Germany who dream of taking over by blood and fire an expanse of territory which ought only to belong to those who labour on it and defend it.[7]

REVOLUTIONARY AWAKENING

This is the major issue with which Guillén feels the writer and intellectual must come to terms:

> A poet, a writer or an intellectual, as a man, has no right, in our times, to sit back in peace; he must take his stand among the ranks of those other men who are not intellectuals but who are working for a noble ideal of a common culture.[8]

For the creative writer, this stand is both a matter of duty and a way of surviving as an artist. Guillén insists that the source of creative energy, "the eternal cell of true art" lies in the depths of the ordinary man's experience - the man in the street or the fields, soldiers, tramps, porters and prostitutes, people who struggle to survive. This is a raw material that feeds and informs his creative writing and provides its revolutionary focus. This firm alignment on the side of the masses implies an open rejection of the pursuit of "pure art" that characterized modernist writing of the later nineteenth and early twentieth centuries. Guillén condemns this purist position which idolized Paris as its spiritual Mecca as a bourgeois sell-out of creativity to the capitalist. The man of letters in the pre-First World War era was "an animal domesticated by the man of financial means"[9] working to satisfy the interests of a class that despised him deep inside. Capitalism then was not only a means of economic production; it had a peculiar means of literary production as well based in the education, orientation and remuneration of the writer in that kind of class society.

The first significant assault on the security of that literary position was the outbreak of the First World War which stirred up reactions that shocked writers into some even more abstruse and isolationist positions such as Dadaism and Surrealism.

The basic economic and literary order had not been effectively shaken. The foundations were still in tact while preparations were being made for the second impending confrontation - the Franco uprising that led to the Spanish Civil War - which proved to be the really effective bombshell as far as intellectuals and writers were concerned. The scandalous barbarism of the Fascist rebels, the tragic death of Federico García Lorca, and the blatant threat to liberty and democracy shocked the sensibility of the most isolated, and catapulted them into the ranks of the revolutionary front. Philosophers, painters, novelists and poets like Julien Benda, Heinrich Mann, and Pablo Neruda joined with Loukol Youcef, Ludmil Stoyanoff, Novemesky, Anderson Nexo, Latika Nakos, Se-U, Jacques Roumain, César Vallejo, Nicolás Guillén, Juan Marinello, Octavio Paz and José Mancisidor in a united and anguished outcry against the inhumanity and barbarism of the "franquistas" (Franco insurgents) and their Italian and German mercenaries.

The contribution of the Spanish Civil War to the revolutionary awakening of Guillén is best understood in the context of the impact of any such traumatic experience among the Spaniards on leading Latin American writers in the twentieth century. Firstly, it was the Spanish-American War of 1895-98 which hurled Rubén Darío from his Modernist "ivory tower" with his purist preoccupations with art for art's sake and drew harsh words of protests against the imperialist activities of the United States at the turn of the century. Secondly, the Spanish Civil War became a crucial turning-point in the experience of Pablo Neruda, César Vallejo and Nicolás Guillén, among others, who were *de facto* witnesses of the Spanish saga. Together they analyzed and bemoaned the horrors of the Civil War and together they symbolized the traumatic effects of the experience in the emotive titles of their poems dedicated to that struggle: *España, en el corazón* (Neruda), *España, a parta de mí este cáliz* (Vallejo) and *España, poema en cuatro anguistas y una esperanza* (Guillén). Guillén's case ought not to be looked at in isolation, since for these three poets in particular, it was a shared response and a common awakening that brought them to the crossroads in their conception of their roles as artists, especially in relation to the dispossessed peoples of Spain and Latin America. It represented for them the discovery of a new commitment to the popular struggle for liberation through world communism.

The case of Pablo Neruda is passionately and convincingly articulated in his long poem (or perhaps better seen as a collection of related poems) "España en el corazón" which appeared in 1937 during the heat of the Spanish Civil War. In the section sub-titled, "Explico algunas cosas" he explains the gruesome reality that shocked him out of his self-insulation:

> And one morning everything was burning,
> and one morning bonfires
> were bursting forth from the earth

devouring living beings,
and from then on, fire,
dust from then on,
and from then on, blood. . .
You will ask why his poetry
does not speak to us of dream, of leaves,
of the great volcanoes of his native land?
Come and see blood in the streets,
come and see
blood in the streets
come and see blood
in the streets![10]

The "conversion" which led Neruda to this new approach to poetry is significant for a man who had always seen the world through the eyes of an anguished and pessimistic recluse whose world of disintegration, broken objects, corrosion, destruction, death and grief held him engrossed in self-contemplation, self-indulgence and self-alienation. The Civil War now led him dramatically into communism, in an experience desribed by Amado Alonso as:

> Not a conversion to God, but to his fellow man, in fact, a genuine conversion in a technical psychological sense: all his spiritual forces both active and dormant, suddenly mobilized and organized with new magnetization, fired with new enthusiasm, justified by and satisfying new goals.[11]

It is this new experience and a new vision of the world and humanity that led him to identify positively with the "People's Army" in the section subtitled, "oda solar al Ejército del Pueblo";

. . .Brothers, go forward,
forward through ploughed lands,
forward in the dry and sleepless night, delirious
and threadbare. . .
. . . .
In the meantime,
root and garland rise out of silence
to await the mineral victory:

every instrument, every red wheel,
every saw handle or plough-share
every extract from the soil, every tremor of blood
wishes to follow your steps, Army of the People:
your organized light reaches the poor
forgotten men, your well defined star
drives its raucous rays into death
and establishes the new eyes of hope.[12]

His poem "Reunión bajo las nuevas banderas" leaves a clear testimony of that conversion. His activities as editor of the journal "Los Poetas del Mundo defienden al Pueblo Español" (1936) and as co-founder (with Vallejo) of "El Grupo Hispanoamericano de Ayuda a España" (1937) reinforce that poetic testimony through concrete action.

The case of Vallejo, though similar, is perhaps less dramatic. Like Neruda he knew intense solitude and deep anguish and pain but these are not always related to mere metaphysical concerns. More often than not the harsh conditions of poverty, strain and poor health lie at the root of his own suffering. This kind of personal experience which is not tinged with inordinate self-indulgence makes it easy for Vallejo to identify with suffering humanity in the struggle for survival. In fact, his poems in *España, aparta de mí este cáliz* (1938) mark the maturing phase of concerns which had been developing in his earlier poetry, *Los heraldos negros* (1918), and in his only novel *Tungsteno* (1931).. From that early stage, Vallejo had identified with the Indian labourers among whom he had grown up, so that the Spanish Civil War served mainly to deepen his basic concern for all suffering humanity. Similarly, his adoption of communism provided not only a possible answer to the socio-economic evils of the world but a faith that brought light and hope in the face of the tragedy of the human condition as he knew it. Refusing to be hamstrung by dogmatism and accepting as his main guide the demands imposed by indigence, hunger and pain, he stands firm in his conviction that the writer must ally himself with the working class and enter into the struggle for justice, brotherhood and solidarity.

Guillén's own reposne to the Spanish Civil War must also be considered against the background of his own ideological development in the years immediately prior to the outbreak of the war. The poet-journalist had really only emerged as a public figure in 1930 with the publication of his dialect poems *Motivos de son* based on the experiences of Negroes in urban slum areas. This publication had been preceded by a series of newspaper articles[13] and one particular poem[14] published in the *Diario De La Marina* in 1929, which opened up a vibrant public debate on the place of the Negro in Cuban society. Alongside distinguished public figures like

Ingeniero Gustavo E. Urrutia and Lino Dou, Guillén was being recognized and watched as a defender of the rights of the Negro and a possible source of constant opposition to reactionary forces in the society. The publication of *Sóngoro Cosongo* (1931) and *West Indies Ltd.* (1934) during the troubled period of popular antipathy to the dictatorship of Machado and the undisguised support he received from the United States, brought Guillén into the spot-light, no longer as a mere debater but as a leading voice in a growing outcry of social protest.

The years 1935 to 1937 were the decisive years in his ideological evolution. At first Guillén accepted a job as a civil servant in the Municipal Dept. of Culture in Havana early in 1935 but found himself progressively moving left politically, that is, contrary to the current of the reactionary government of Carlos Mendieta which was closing down leftist newspapers published by the Communist Party of Cuba and the Anti-imperialist League of Cuba. In the meantime Guillén the civil servant was being invited to serve on the Editorial Boards of the Communist Party journal, RESUMEN (April 1935) and the marxist writers' journal, MEDIODIA (June, 1936).

The open split came in August 1936 when Guillén lost his job because of his involvement in anti-government demosntrations. His arrest, brief imprisonment and trial for "subversive and pornographic" activities left no one in doubt as to his real ideological position. This became more fully enunciated in his next book of poems, *Cantos para soldados y sones para turistas* (1937) in which he consolidated an already militant stand adopted in *West Indies Ltd.* A revolutionary outlook emerges in his call for soldiers to rejoin the ranks of the working class and turn their arms on the forces of oppression. The protest songs become far too virulent to be used for purposes of entertainment. They are bitter songs that rise from the depths of the "cancerous guts" of the shanty-town folk from the "solar".

It is at this stage that Guillén looks to Spain and the crisis of the Fascist uprising with all its atrocities. The picture he has gathered from as far away as Cuba and Mexico is one that stirs him to write the touching poems entitled: *España, Poema en cuatro angustias y una esperanza* (May 1937) - a work which synthesises the main thrust of the Latin American response to the painful struggle of the popular, republican movement in Spain to withstand the onslaught of the Fascists. In them he captures the anguished saga of a heroic people being torn apart by demonic forces. He, in dramatic empathy, now shares the anguish and horror that shook Neruda out of his cell and sealed Vallejo's destiny with the proletariat.

What Guillén has done, better than the rest, is to apprehend and express in forceful and emotive imagery, the sentimental, "gut" connection of Latin Americans to the Spanish people:

The root of my tree, twisted;
the root of my tree, of your tree,
of all our trees,
drinking blood, moist blood,
the root of my tree, of your tree.
I can feel it...
nailed into the depths of my earth
nailed there, nailed,
dragging me and lifting me and speaking to me,
shouting to me.[15]

When he finally turns towards Spain raising his voice of hope and optimism, and in clear lyrical tones declares his unequivocal call for revolution, he is not engaging in mere rhetoric. His pen is his weapon in the hard struggle alongside miners, muleteers, bartenders, prisoners, waterfront workers, labourers and soldiers. It is not to be overlooked that in that same year, in the height of the Spanish Civil War, Guillén, while still in Spain, was admitted to full membership of the Communist Party of Cuba.

REVOLUTIONARY MILITANCY

This alliance of intellectuals and artists with the proletariat marks the dawning of a new level of awareness and the acceptance of a non-bourgeois conception of the role of the artist and thinker in the society. The idea of political militancy as a dimension of literary activity becomes a credo based on the conviction that all human experience, and especially that of "the people", forms the cultural sediment that gives art its vitality and validity. This credo expresses itself in action and not just in empty rhetoric or mere professions of sympathy:

A "sympathetic" stance is not enough;
direct effort is essential; lukewarm
support which does not put anything at
stake is not sufficient; rather what
is required is active, dynamic militancy
which risks everything, sacrifices everything,
offers everything and gives everything.[16]

That ideological alignment takes on greater import than a mere liberal stand for democracy and justice. It has a clear socialist dimension almost of doctrinaire proportions which underpins a strong revolutionary intent. This comment on the world situation in the forties and the people's understanding of the forces at work against their interests elucidates the ideological position by giving an almost textbook assessment of an international revolutionary situation:

> ...the contradictions of the capitalist
> mode of production have become so acute,
> the conflicts among the different bands
> of "gangsters" anxious to share up the
> planet amongst themselves, so obvious,
> and the scandals of that shambles of a
> family, with all its defects and vices,
> called the bourgeoisie, so grave and
> frequent, that in the end, there was no
> way of preventing the police from appearing
> and the neighbourhood from being fully
> aprised...They (the people) know very
> well what class of interests, alien to
> the real popular interest, motivates those
> pantomimes in France as much as in England,
> in Germany just as in Italy, and in the
> United States as well as in Cuba.[17]

International confrontation is viewed in the somewhat Manichean terms of the humane revolutionaries versus a savage Nazi-fascist imperialist alliance. The former group comprises the socialists, communists, liberals and the world proletariat whereas the second grouping is that of the capitalist-imperialist interest led by the Nazi-fascist front and supported by a powerful conservative bourgeois class. As he himself says of the struggle in Spain:

> As one can see, it is a question of two
> spirits, two mentalities that are diametrically
> opposed. On one side, there is
> the old Spanish nobility of spirit which
> treats the fortunes of war with the purest
> elements of mercy; on the other side there
> is the brutal blindness of the savage, the
> bloody impetus of Fascism which closes its
> eyes to anything that might stem the
> absolute rule of force.[18]

Guillén's interpretation of this international struggle therefore offers, at times, an idealistic and sentimental quality which no doubt grew out of his deep faith in the people and their capacity for struggle and endurance as well as his conviction that the capitalist order was rapidly disintegrating. Whether history eventually proved him wrong or not, he shared the confidence and faith in imminent victory of Lieutenant-Colonel Modesto and the people of Madrid and Barcelona of whom he says that "they have enough courage to resist and rise to the height of their destiny".[19] He left no possibility for the Nazi and Fascist devils to win, either against the Russian resistance or the Popular Front in Spain. It was tantamount to refusing to admit the possible triumph of evil over good. Even in his treatment of the Soviet attitude to culture and human progress he left no room for possible persecution or muzzling of freedom of expression and creativity. That kind of philistine activity was restricted to the Nazi and Fascist camps. Justifiable as this view of the Soviet Union as a peace-loving, culture-conscious and creative people might have been in the early forties, from the vantage point of the seventies and onwards its idealism becomes readily questionable.

This idealism however seemed essential to the revolutionary action needed to change the world order, particularly on the American scene. The situation in the Americas was ripe for revolution - the abdominable lynching of Negroes in the United States, the deplorable rule of Stenio Vincent in Haiti, political crimes and conservative dominance in Colombia, saltpetre in Chile and sugar in the West Indies and Cuba. These all "breed the same popular grief, the same anguish, the same misery and, fortunately, they also give rise to the same rebellion".[20] This is Guillén's basis for an effective revolutionary struggle - the recognition of the weaknesses and evils of an inimical system combined with the idealism and passion for a militant drive for change:

> This is to say, we shall fight as long
> as there is an injustice to correct in
> Cuba; we will show the people who are
> the terrible democrats that lynch Negroes
> in the South and slander and condemn
> communists in the North; we shall ask
> for the freedom of Albizu Campos day
> after day so that he can continue fighting
> for the liberation of Puerto Rico; we will
> defend our country until it is free of
> enemies from outside and inside, Fascists
> who dream of converting it into a Hitlerian
> fief, national traitors acting as accomplices,
> kneeling before the foreigner.[21]

This is the militant spirit that produces the political satire of 1949 and 1952-53. Here he takes a firm stand against Batista's attempt to hoodwink the masses into accepting his empty pretensions of a protective and progressive democracy and underscores the horrors of repression in a context where hunger, poor housing, low wages, poor sanitation, exploitation and dispossession can give rise to seething protest and revolutionary activity.

To deal with this provocative and explosive situation Guillén, the journalist-activist, took recourse to lampoon, ridicule, caricature and at times almost reached the point of virulence and acrimony in his satirical "décimas" and "coplas". It was the kind of open confrontation in the newspapers that left no stones unturned in the public eye and which was intended to damage the image of the successive corupt and repressive Governments of Carlos Prio Socrarrás and Fulgencio Batista. The price of such journalistic militancy was the closure of the communist newspaper HOY edited by Guillén in 1949 and the poetic-journalist's exile from 1953 to 1959. That kind of incisive prose and satirical poetry were, in the eyes of the wounded parties, no less subversive and dangerous than the physical attack on the Moncada barracks in 1953.

Like the popular singers whose voices rise from amongst the silent masses that patiently bear the yoke, Guillén looks ahead with an optimistic, revolutionary vision and foresees the day of reckoning when the heedless explioters will be hung by the anguished songs of the sufferers:

> I say this to you for these are terrible
> symptoms in these songs. In them is
> embodied the presentiment that in the
> surly tameness of those people who hear
> the voice of the singer there throbs,
> unnoticed, an intense but unexpressed
> anguish. Sometimes, in the fiery heat of
> the harsh Antillean sun, it is likely to
> be the sugar cane and coffee labourer who
> bites his certain anger as he toils bending
> over the earth; at other times, it may
> be the man born under the sign of cotton
> in the yankee south, in the bloody south
> of Jim Crow and Lynch where Negroes die
> burnt, tortured, abused, harrassed, hanged,
> with their bodies resounding tragically
> like bells over the jokes of their assassins.
> Jazz and the "son" burst forth in tears and

> grind their teeth with music, waiting for
> the first day of judgement when the syncopated
> rhythm will coil around the neck of the
> oppressor. The hangmen dance around uncon-
> cerned; they dance beneath the yellow light
> of their whips, the green light of their hatred,
> the red light of their bonfires, the blue light
> of poison gas, the violet-coloured light of
> their own putrefaction... They dance merrily
> over the corpses of their victims, but they
> will not escape their vengence.[22.]

For Guillén, the Negro, and particularly the Negro of the Americas and the Caribbean, has a special role to play in the militant avantguard of the revolutionary struggle:

> No one is anti-fascist like the Negro
> and few like the Cuban Negro, because
> he knows that the very root of Fascism
> grows out of terrain fertilized by
> racial hatred and the division of men
> into inferior and superior beings and
> that he, the Negro, has been assigned
> the lowest place... The Negro, moreover,
> comprises the majority of the enslaved
> labouring class, and as such is painfully
> tied to the dismal economic process of
> that semi-colonial society now being
> exploited by North American imperialism.[23]

This explains the leading role by Negroes in the militant Trade Union Movement of the forties - Lázaro Peña, Aracelio Iglesias, and Jesús Menédez - on the docks and in the sugar belt.

Guillén sees his personal commitment to struggle as being inevitable. It represents a deep personal sense of destiny in his role as a writer and in his character as a Cuban and a black man:

> I wish then to affirm here and now a
> triple cause for my support for the
> Spanish people: as a writer, because

> I am convinced that no one can be a self-respecting writer without utilizing his talent in the defense of culture; as a Cuban, because my country is also engaged in a struggle against Fascism represented by a minority which enslaves and exploits it, and which has the same character of those who rose up in arms against the legitimate Government of Spain; and as a Negro, because Fascism implies a check to the universalisation of the human spirit, a blocking of the diffusion of the purest democratic principles and a stupid return to old stages which are being overcome continuously by processes of development in the society.[24.]

This fervent militancy permeates his prose, his speeches, his poetry. In large measure, it represents the militant spirit of the youth and the revolutionary avantguard in the difficult years of the forties and fifties. Not even the success of the Cuban Revolution cooled that fiery spirit, for the poet-journalist recognized that until the cause of the Chilean people, or that of the Negroes of the United States, or the struggle of Asian peoples, is over, his struggle in defence of culture and humanity is never ended.

NOTES

[1]. Spain - 1937-1938; South America - 1937, 1945-1948.

[2] Nicolás Guillén, *Prosa de prisa*, La Habana, 1975, pp. 139-140.

[3] Ibid. p. 150.

[4] Ibid. pp. 232-233.

[5] Ibid. p. 359.

[6] Ibid. p. 237.

[7] Ibid. pp. 107-108.

[8] Ibid. p. 151.

[9] Ibid. p. 147.

[10] Pablo Neruda, *Tercera Residencia* (Buenos Aires, 1961) pp. 46-47.

[11] Amado Alonso, *Poesía y estilo de Pablo Neruda*, (Buenos Aires, 1968) pp. 348-349.

[12] Neruda, op. cit. pp. 69-70.

[13] "El camino de Harlem" (April 21); "La conquista del blanco" (May 5); "El blanco: he aquí el problema" (June 9).

[14] "Pequeña oda a Kid Chocolate" (December 29).

[15] Nicolás Guillén, *Obra Poética*, Vol. I, pp. 210-211.

[16] Nicolás Guillén, *Prosa de prisa*, op. cit. p. 102.

[17] Ibid. p. 146.

[18] Ibid. p. 122.

[19] Ibid. p. 123.

[20] Ibid. p. 344.

[21] Ibid. p. 162.

[22] Ibid. p. 347.

23 Ibid. p. 85.

[24] Ibid.

CHAPTER SIX

THE QUESTION OF RACE

To understand the position of Nicolás Guillén on the question of race in twentieth-century Cuba, it is important to examine his prose and poetry jointly and to bear in mind, always, the revolutionary orientation of his adult writing. The former is important for the completeness of vision it provides and the latter for the cohesive focus it brings to a controversial and often misrepresented point of view.

To know the poet and not the jounalist is to know only one small corner of a rich and perceptive mind. It is Guillén himself who made the confession: "I am a jounalist first and a poet after...Jounalism is, for me, an outlet through which I free myself of many things that I cannot express in verse; not to mention that there are many of my poems whose style is distinctly journalistic and familiar."[1] Surely, Guillén the chronicler, reporter and interviewer, the political analyst and literary critic, the social commentator and militant revolutionary is best known through his prose writings.[2] His poetry is, in fact, complementary to his prose. The latter forms the matrix - the statement of facts, the objective analysis, the supplier of material for the inventive imagination; the former is the woven fabric, the imaginative interpretation, the creative extract.

In general, Guillén's prose seems to develop along the same basic lines as his poetry, both being profoundly influenced by socio-political trends in Cuba and the Caribbean as well as international big-stick politics, and both being informed by a personal view of history and culture, by personal travels and study, personal encounters and a deep personal concern for humanity.

RACE AND RACISM

The earliest phase of his prose manifests a basic preoccupation with race and racial attitudes in Cuba and therefore relates directly to the poems of the early thirties - *Motivos De Son* (1930) and *Songoro Cosongo* (1931). In fact, his first article of significant resonance "Camino de Harlem" ("Road to Harlem") appeared on April 21, 1929 in "Ideales de una raza", a special Sunday section of the newspaper *Diario De L Marina*. This almost coincided with the writing of his first poem on the Negro theme, "Pequeña oda a Kid Chocolate"[3] published on December 29, 1929, in the same newspaper. These two cogent expressions of black consciousness did not come by chance and are not to be dismissed lightly. They grew out of hard personal experience and years of psychological conditioning in the harsh realities of racial prejudice in Cuba prior to the Revolution. This he made clear in an interview when he said:

> From childhood I got accustomed to fighting against racial prejudice...I witnessed the spectacle of discrimination against Negroes because of the colour of their skin and against more than a few whites on account of their social background. This made me rebellious against that kind of society and out of that rebelliousness sprang my opposition not only to racial prejudice but to all other forms of prejudice.[4]

Besides, Guillén's activities among the Negro Societies of Camagüey in the twenties made him one of the more popular and notable black activists in Cuba even before he was 25. He was closely associated with the militant cultural and social thrust of Societies like the "Maceo" and the "Victoria" and with prominent black journalists and activists like Gustavo E. Urrutia, Lino D`ou and Felix Nápoles, among others. He was one of the founders of the black magazine LIS that appeared in January, 1923, whose main objective was to project the activities and objectives of the Negro Societies in Camagüey and "fight against racial discrimination as practised not only by whites against Negroes - a very marked practice in those days -, but also among mulattoes and Negroes, a very curious phenomenon with its natural economic explanation".[5]

SENSE OF MISSION

Arising out of this background is a distinct impression that from very early in his career, Guillén saw himself as a missionary with a specific calling to vindicate the cause of the Negro and mulatto in Cuba. This profound sense of mission firmly contradicts the accusation that his earliest poetry on the Negro theme tended to be comical, frivolous and picturesque. Any such negative comment on *Motivos de son* based on its picturesque scenes, its direct social realism, its use of dialect forms and its treatement of attitudes and relationships in slum areas, loses sight of the poignant message of protest, the penetrating insights into the psychology of poverty and survival and the tragedy of dispossession which arise out of those early poems of strong racial passion. Whatever line Guillén followed subsequently, it remains clear that a strong note of racial feeling (as distinct from racial prejudice) prompted his *Motivos de son*; and this racial feeling was intimately linked with a sense of duty and commitment to the cause of the Negro in a strictly national context.

As early as April, 1929, prior to any of his "black" poetry, Guillén affirmed this calling declaring that "that is the present duty of the intelligent Negro youth of Cuba - to follow in the footsteps of Juan Gualberto Gómez[6] who carried on his shoulders the dual task of fighting for the political independence of his country and of elevating the position of his race, the Negro race, in political and social spheres".[7]

Guillén's own answer to the challenge raised by Gómez and other Negro mentors such as Lino D'ou is a positive and militant stand for struggle on the part of the Negro:

> The answer is serious but nevertheless, it must be given. Surely, the coloured race in Cuba still has a problem and still needs to fight to have it resolved. Equality has not been extended to all sectors of life in our Republic; there are still many trenches, prematurely deserted, where it is necessary to continue fighting against innumerable prejudices.
> (April, 1929)[8]

BLACK AWARENESS AND RACIAL CLEAVAGE

In spite of numerous attempts by observers to minimise the extent of racial sentiment in Guillén's poetry, it seems clear that the Negro cause, particularly at that stage, was not conceived purely in terms of a dispossessed proletariat, and without any firm racial consideration. The case he presents is a specific one of an ethnic group coming to terms with itself and with the whole society at a point in time that Guillén describes as "The crossroads of its destiny".[9] At the crossroads, the Negro has a specific challenge which brings him into open confrontation with the white Cuban community:

> To fight? Not at all. To remind them that we are in fact their brothers. To let them know they have to deal with us. To make them aware that we live in the Republic of Cuba and not a southern cotton plantation in the United States. (May, 1929)[10]

As Guillén puts it, the whites have become quite accustomed to being alone in the frontline of national life, mainly through the apathy of the Negroes, so that the time is ripe for the blacks to take the whites by surprise and suddenly appear where they are least expected to be seen.

The cleavage is expressed here in unequivocal, racial terms - "they" and "us" - and is being seen from a black nationalist's viewpoint. Although open racial conflict did not seem to be very strong, racial discrimination and prejudice were realities which had to be faced and eliminated. Guillén himself vividly describes the problem of segragation in national parks in his article, "Road to Harlem" and underscores the explosive potential of that social division. This was not just a problem in parks in Cienfuegos and Camagüey but it extended to barbershops, dance schools and jobs in Havana. It was the kind of situation which exploded later in the city of Trinidad in January, 1934 when Negroes decided to invade those sections of the Central Park habitually reserved for whites, and were met with hostility.

It is in this situation of social cleavage based on race and class that Guillén's early writing naturally found its mainspring. This explains, in large measure, the black-white counter-balance attempted in his "Pequeña oda a Kid Chocolate" where the triumphant Negro boxer, in the face of white envy, now "understands himself as a Negro" and "really speaks in Negro". It also explains why in "Ayé me dijeron negro" the black man retorts bitterly against any suggestion that mulattoes or whites are better than he is; or why in "Negro bembón" the black man will no longer be angry when he is called a thick-lipped Negro; or, why, in "Mi chiquita", the black man in the slums is so proud of his black mistress who cooks, sews, washes and irons so well; or why in "Mulata" the Negro declares his distinct preference for his Negro woman even over the mulatto woman in spite of the obvious sexuality of the latter.

There is no doubt that this represents a level of racial consciousness at both the societal and personal levels, which Guillén needed to explore, interpret and channel. The literary *vogue* ("moda") of the twenties which was sparked off by European artists and thinkers like Paul Morand, Blaise Cendrars and Leo Frobenius in their new zeal for Negro art, and followed through by white Cubans like Alejo Carpentier, José Zacarías Tallet and Ramón Güirao or by the Puerto Rican, Luis Palés Matos, between 1926 and 1928, became, by 1930, in the words of Guillén himself, a vital *method* ("modo") of dealing with endemic national problems. As he said in his prologue to *Sóngoro Cosongo*, "I am not unaware of the fact that these verses will be repugnant to many persons, because they deal with issues concerning Negroes and the people, but that does not matter to me. Rather, I am happy."[11]

Guillén categorically dismisses the mere literary fad as circumstancial tourism which never penetrated deeply into the human tragedy of the race, being more like excursions organised for photographing coconut trees, drums and naked

Negroes, whilst there existed the seething drama of the flesh and blood Negro bearing the scars of whiplashes, a Negro now fused with the whites to produce an indelible mulatto imprint on the Cuban social scene.[12]

What Guillén needed to work out was his own method of dealing with that historical drama and its social and cultural ramifications, and to do this he needed to use both poetry and journalism. His approach is to use his prose to examine the realities critically whilst in his poetry he pursues an ideal of harmony by creating models that fit in with his dreams for the future and his vision of a historical experience of black-white interaction and intermingling. Essays such as "Camino de Harlem" form an unquestionable base for the poetic models of racial synthesis expressed in "Balada de los dos abuelos", "Dos niños", "Son número 6", "Puente" and the satirical treatment of racial prejudice which emerges from "El abuelo", "Canción del bongó" and "Ayé me dijeron negro" is their logical corollary.

THE RATIONAL APPROACH

The first line of attack is to seek to foster honesty and frankness on all sides as a prerequisite for human understanding and social harmony. He is obviously working towards a level of honest exchange between blacks and whites which could only be made possible by "convincing ourselves that we do not like one another as much as we say we do and applying ourselves to the noble task of acting just a little like Cubans, substituting artificial embraces and banderoles with mutual respect and definite understanding."[13]

In dealing with prejudice and hostility from the whites, Guillén never makes the mistake of losing his poise through emotional excesses. His tools in the struggle are sound logic and rationality coupled with a mild touch of irony, but always with a view to achieving understanding rather than creating pain. He takes a firm and unwavering stand against bland generalisations which in fact cover up subtle prejudices. He rejects the argument put forward by educated whites that "the problem of the Cuban Negro is simply cultural", implying that educational achievement is the Negro's exclusive passport to acceptability.[14] He vehemently opposes the views of the white Cuban sociologist, Ramino Cabrera, on: the inferiority of the Negro race, separate education for blacks and whites, and the absence of any black influence on the whites of Cuba.[15] He objects to patronising gestures which see in the Negro's dancing talent his only gift of the spirit, "as if always to see his soul in his feet",[16] or which see in the Negro's role in literature as a purely burlesque decoration or a curio.[17]

The opportunity is never lost to pick up the most subtle sign of conscious or unconscious racism. With a characteristic, wry smile, Guillén would narrate anecdotes through which his own highly sensitive internal radar system picks up the racist currents that some whites nurture ingenuously in their breast. In one instance, a young writer declares his willingness to invite the poet to dinner at his home, but winces at the surprising reciprocation of the invitation. In another instance, a politician boasts of his egalitarian beliefs but winds up his oratory affirming his preference for a poor black man over a rich white man. Instead of reacting angrily Guillén chooses to retort with tongue in cheek and with measured tolerance and understanding.

His stand on negative Negro attitudes is equally frank and reprehensive, a fact that gives his stand some balance. When he attacks the hypocrisy of whites who, when in the çompany of Negroes, grudgingly admit that the Negro is their brother, he also criticises the blacks who would acknowledge the whites as friends only when they are in their presence. He further blames the Negro for the timidity, vanity and apathy which cause him to isolate himself from the whites and to admit any kind of inferiority. This, in his view is a social sickness that the whites have been aware of and have accepted and manipulated, and which the blacks themselves have encouraged by their lack of aggressiveness.

IDENTITY, RACE AND CULTURE

At no stage is Guillén in doubt about his identity and the racial component of his understanding of himself as an individual. He is first and foremost a black man and a Cuban - the two conditions that lie at the centre of his consciousness and his sense of destiny. In his historic address to the International Congress of Writers in Madrid in July 1937, Guillén declared:

> I come to you as a black man, but, paradoxically,
> I do not come with a discriminatory, exclusive
> racial concept of blackness. Rather, I am here to
> remind you that the Negro's position as outcast is
> his most powerful human driving force, a force which
> hurls him forward towards a wider horizon that is
> more universal, more just, towards a horizon for which
> all honourable men are struggling today.[18]

To Guillén, this sharp consciousness of a black identity is not used as a pedestal or a launching pad for aggressive racialism. Confident as he is about his blackness and black identification, Guillén abhors racism which he sees as a narrow and debasing sentiment that robs the individual of his stature as a man, and the community of its potentiality for human development and progress:

> There is, in that feeling of racial superiority,
> an effective pose, a show of impotence, fear and

> cowardice in the face of social progress, progress which has taught us, from the cave to the present time, that it can only be achieved by means of a growing universalisation of the spirit and an increasing flexibility in human relations.[19]

Guillén argues that this problem of racism is closely related to considerations of class, and that racialism is the distinct preserve of the bourgeoisie who are the real enemies of human progress. In the lower strata of society, blacks and whites fraternise in their common socio-economic plight. At the top, the national heroes and outstanding intellectual and political figures rise above that narrowness of mind and meanness of spirit that is characteristic of racialism. It is the petty, egotistical professionals, businessmen, artisans and clerical workers who entertain such vulgar thoughts and sentiments as part of the bourgeois mentality of a capitalist system that must find debasing criteria for stratifying society in the interest of a privileged class.

This explains why Guillén's idea of the mulatto nature of the national identity is not just a question of the confluence of two racial streams. The mulatto image is built up as a spiritual and cultural phenomenon in which the Cuban Negro is thoroughly hispanicised and the white Cuban unmistakably africanised, and treated as a means of undermining the superiority complexes of the white bourgeoisie, a kind of antidote to racism and exploitation:

> Above all, our social divisions are reduced to a common denominator - that is the spirit. Cuba does not have a black spirit nor a white spirit and for that reason there is not the kind of racial militancy which pits two opposing groups against each other in a fiery exchange.
>
> For me...the question of race is ambitious and circular. It entails organising oneself for battle on clearly defined fronts...Race is an army ...We Cubans get our colour from inside and not outside...Here, we are all somewhat mulatto deep within us and it won't be long before we will show it at skin level.[20]

Elsewhere, he reiterates this view of acculturation in terms of mutual cultural imputs:

> I was born in a country, Cuba, where the Negro represents a very important sector of the population

> to whose spiritual formation he has contributed,
> from the depths of three hundred years of slavery,
> elements which are easily recognisable in the
> national psychology...The Cuban Negro is also
> *Spanish* because along with ignominious marks of
> slavery, he received and assimilated the elements
> of that culture...[21]

Guillén's whole approach is to resolve the racial question from three different angles. Firstly, over and above the question of pigmentation, he raises and develops the concept of the "colour from inside", the spiritual dimension that is blind to colour and that recognises and relates to humanity as the only race. Now this is his universal answer, the universal ideal, a position that is reminiscent of José Martí's views on race: man has no special rights because he belongs to a particular race; say man and that implies all the rights; whites and blacks who speak of "their race"" are being redundant; anything that divides or categorises men is a sin against humanity; humanity is more than white, mulatto or black, to be Cuban is to be more than white, mulatto or black.

The second solution may be called the national answer, the national ideal of a mulatto culture ("negri-blanca" as he describes it). This is a concept that does not seem to make any allowance for cultural pluralism, nor symbiosis, nor diversity based on social, racial and cultural origins. It makes no allowances for minority groups and their peculiarities. The Chinese, for example, late-comers in comparison with whites and blacks, no doubt lose their particularity and become assimilated into the dominant national cultural complex. What Guillén is postulating is a unique, effective, mulatto synthesis which represents a homogeneous national culture, and which does not even suggest the possibility of regional variations. This cultural unity he extols as another experience of the spirit with profound and mysterious implications for the individual psyche of each Cuban and for the national identity. To him, this creole amalgam is the unquestionable result of a dialectical experience experience with a depth of four hundred years, so that he is confident that it exists as a socio-anthropological reality:

> The Cuban spirit is *mestizo* and from the spirit
> outwards the definitive colour will come towards
> the skin.[22]

Admittedly, Guillén's version must be regarded as a poetic vision and an intuitive evaluation rather than a scientific conclusion, but it serves as a firm base for his ardent nationalism. This becomes a possible alternative to the racialism of colonial society as well as an antidote to the cultural and social stratifications and biases of the old plantation economy.

His third angle of approach is to diminsh the importance of racial difference and racial consciousness as social issues of moment and to promote the pursuits of humanist values such as freedom, justice and solidarity in struggle as the binding forces for the Cubans of the forties and fifties.[23] The revolutionary aspirations of blacks, mulattoes and whites, the burden of oppression and exploitation under local dictaroships and foreign capitalists experienced by all ethnic groups in the lower strata of the society and shared by conscientious and sensitive intellectuals, are issues that supersede all parochial preoccupations and prejudices even if they do not eliminate them totally. This is the revolutionary answer. To fall back into racial affirmations would be, for him, a retrograde step that would highlight differences rather than explore common bonds or common grounds for solidarity.

For Cubans of the sixties and seventies, Guillén believes firmly that the problem of race has died with the advent of the Revolution:

> "In the countries where a revolution has taken place, as in Cuba, the problem of negritude does not make sense, because it would be a kind of racism...But when a revolution erases that struggle and gives power to the working class without any regard for skin colour, the concept of racial superiority does not exist any more."[24]

NEGRITUDE

This is why the Guillén of the Revolutionary era has declared his unwillingness to be identified with the concept of "negritude" either as an ideology or as a literary movement. He recognises in negritude the potential to undermine the three models he has defended as valid interpretations of the Cuban experience - the spiritual model, the mulatto model and the revolutionary model -, and is therefore only willing to concede any validity to negritude "in countries where there is a black population exploited by a white colonial sector" and where it develops as one manifestation of the class struggle "linked to movements of national liberation".[25]

Now, whatever Guillén's forward-looking revolutionary view might be, one does not lose sight of the fact that his own position in the thirties and forties and even up to his remarkable family elegy, "El apellido" (1954) approximated very closely to that of other leading exponents of "negritude" in the Caribbean:

> The blacks find it necessary to strive to expose their cultural values: their music, their sculpture, their painting, and so on... In Cuba itself, before the Revolution, an emphasis on blackness was explainable

> because the artistic, political, cultural, indeed the human, values of the black man had to be stressed in the face of discrimination or slavery; and one had to give emphasis to this element in the national culture.[26]

In some ways this coincides with the views of Césaire expressed in an interview with Sonia Aratán and René Depestre:

> Senghor and I took the intiative in this movement ("negritude") which would enable the black man to become aware of himself": we are not French, we are not English; it is absurd to think of ourselves as black Frenchmen. We are, first of all, Negroes. It was a way of affirming our fidelity to Mother Africa, a way of reasserting Negro values, an attempt to recover the good and the valid that subsisted in the Negro past...In my view, it was a kind of weapon for combatting cultural and political oppression.[27]

One baisc difference between these two Caribbean poets, however, is that Césaire continues to stress his blackness and his Negro heritage as an essential dimension of his being and of his understanding of his historical reality whereas Guillén disregards the idea of blackness as an important factor once the colonial class problem is eliminated. Césaire insists that the political aspect of his reality does not override or eliminate his basic condition as a Negro, nor does Marxist theory answer the Negro's problem adequately. The emancipation of the Negro has to mean more than a mere political liberation, for the Negro has certain historical peculiarities (experience, history, culture, problems) which form the basis of his sense of identification and solidarity. It is these particularities that need to be explored in depth, rather than to be ignored or rejected, if the Negro is to discover and develop a full universal dimension.

Without being racialist, therefore, Césaire has adhered to a positive and creative racial line that affirms his refusal to be engulfed in European theories and abstractions - be they surrealistic, Marxist, Leninist or otherwise. Guillén on the other hand has adopted a clear Marxist-Leninist position that not only rejects racialism *per se* as a weakness and a divisive factor, but sees the whole question of racial identity as insignificant in the face of the wider Marxist concept of class struggle.

For him, the Marxist position is a more advanced stage of struggle and solidarity than "negritude" whose relevance in the Third World is restricted to those areas which have not experienced a Revolution in the Marxist sense:

> Now, I believe that negritude can be explained as the struggle of oppressed and dispossessed black people against imperialism as represented by North Americans, the French, English and Dutch; that is to say, by white men who oppress, alienate and dispossess them, as in Africa. The same thing happens in the Lesser Antilles, especially in Guadeloupe and Martinique.[28]

Now Guillén's position might be understandable in the Cuban context not only because of the Revolution, but also because Negroes are a minority group and because people like Fernando Ortiz, Martí and Guillén himself have been expounding, for years, that the Cuban national identity is a mulatto synthesis that supersedes all racial boundaries and peculiarities.

This surely helps to explain why Marxist critics like Rachid and René Depestre have declared themselves firmly in support of the same non-racial, "revolutionary" line adopted by Guillén. The only form of "negritude" that seems acceptable to Depestre is that "which completes the articulation of Marxism to our West Indian realities, adding to it the knowledge of our historical uniqueness and, consequently, the traumatic experience of slavery, colonisation and racism...that (which) lives the socialist experience more intensely than the racial experience and which fights so that everywhere, an end will be put to the epidermal interpretation of the historical situation of men as colionalism has done in the case of Negroes."[29]

When Depestre says that negritude should outline "to black peoples their duty to carry out the revolution in order to be able to affirm their identity in world history", it must be understood that, like Guillén, he has ruled out any question of racial identity. The predominant and definitive factor rests with the "socio-economic development peculiar to each of our peoples"-:

> It becomes evident, after analysis, that belonging to the same race, or the colour of the skin or the shape of the nose or lips, or the 'diaspora' which resulted from the slave trade, are not the factors which determine the national character of each of our islands, but rather the concrete conditions of life in each islands, the conditions of historical development which belong to each West Indian community.[30]

Césaire, however, notwithstanding his Marxist sympathies and revolutionary zeal, takes a different line in the context of the French West Indies where Negroes are in the majority and where the assertion of one's Negro identification is still a vital form of resistance to French assimilation. National character and national identity are not determined merely by the prevailing socio-economic conditions. Historical development means more than the dialectical processes of historical change, and more than a theoretical or actual class struggle. For Césaire, there are cultural and racial perspectives at the centre of the struggle of black peoples in the Caribbean for self-identification and self-determination. These factors are decisive indices in any revolutionary praxis that is geared to remove all forms of alienation and assimilation. They are crucial to any definition of "our historical uniqueness" even in " the historical context of the Revolution in the Third World". (Depestre)

Césaire remains adamant in this view that " we are Negroes with numerous historical peculiarities"[31] and although he does not specify these "spiritual and mental characteristics", he seems to stand firmly against any movement or ideology that tries to absorb the black man into a universal context without recognising, emphasising and exploring his particularities. This tendency he regards as a dangerous process of assimilation and depersonalisation which could rob the Negro of his creative and productive potential. To him, then, negritude becomes both a political and a cultural weapon. It is a form of resistance, but it is also an integrating force for black peoples in the contemporary world.

INTEGRATION

The nature of this integrating process is another factor that separates Césaire and Guillén. Césaire on the one hand, without trying to formulate vain dogmas and, surely, without engaging in the kind of mystification that has provoked René Depestre, G.R. Coulthard and Rachid,[32] has seen the Negro's history as an experience that reaches back as far as his pre-Caribbean or pre-Middle Passage experience, in Africa. When Césaire says that, "There is no negritude that is predetermined, no substance, (but that) there is a history, a history that has been lived, "he is not thinking purely of the class struggle in the Caribbean between the white colonialist and imperialist powers and the exploited Negroes. He is also talking about an experience that he describes as "fidelity to Mother Africa" and the heritage drawn from that matrix. When he talks of a "return to the sources" he is dealing with a cultural process that leads all black people to relate their African past to their own contemporary experience in a dynamic way that establishes and solidifies their consciousness of common identification, common struggle and common revolutionary destiny. This he seems to accept as one pathway to the reintegration of a sense of wholeness and of belonging without the error of abstracting "essences". He is obviously drawing a clear line between mystifying notions of the virtue of blackness as a colour and blackness as a determining factor in the concreteness of an experience of history and of traditions lost or retained.

Guillén, on the other hand, sees integration in the Cuban context as a bi-focal experience shaped solely by Cuban history. Firstly there is the hispanicisation of the Negro and his integration into a national mulatto mould which is the product of a history that Guillén restricts to the local setting. He refuses to go back in history any further than the landing on Cuban shores or at best, the Middle Passage. As "El apellido" indicates very plainly, any connections beyond that point become nebulous and painful to recall.

Secondly, the Revolution is seen not only as an alternate integrating force but as the dominant and decisive factor in the long process of interaction, adaptation and integration. Guillén has maintained that the problem of race "had only one solution, that is the Revolutionary solution, since the disappearnce of classes would lead to the ending of the division of the Cuban society into races."[33]

Now, to those who have not lived through that Revolutionary experience, the change might seem rather sudden for a problem of such endemic proportions and such varying nuances. One might even get the impression of revolutionary idealism overriding pragmatism. But then, Guillén now speaks from a vantage point inside a Revolution that theoretically and ideologically endorses his own models and which progressively seeks to transform those visions into concrete reality. He cannot be accused of betraying the Negro whose cause he has espoused and articulated for over fifty years. His Negro has simply lost his "negritude" and become fully assimilated into a tight national destiny and a fixed national ideal.

NOTES

[1] "Conversación con Nicolás Guillén" in *Recopilación de textos sobre* Nicolás Guillén, (CASA, 1972, p.55).

[2] Nicolás Guillén, *Prosa de prisa* (crónicas), Universidad Central de Las Villas, 1962; Prosa de prisa: 1929-1972, (Tomo I), Editorial Arte y Literatura, La Habana, 1975. *Prosa de prisa: 1929-1972* (Tomo II), Editorial Arte y Literatura, La Habana, 1976.

[3] The black Cuban boxer, Eligio Sardiñas who was a sensational figure on the international scene in 1929.

[4] "Conversación con Nicolás Guillén" in *Recopilación de textos sobre Nicolás Guillén*, op. cit., pp 50-51.

[5] Ibid. p. 37.

[6] Negro thinker, journalist and political activist of the late 19th and early 20th centuries who fought for full independence rather than partial autonomy or annexation for Cuba, and total redemption (social, political, spiritual and economic) for the Negro.

[7] Nicolás Guillén, *Prosa de prisa,* Vol I, op. cit. p. 3.

[8] Ibid.

[9] Ibid. p. 35.

[10] Ibid. p. 9.

[11] In *Obra poética*, Vol. I, pp. 113-114.

[12] *Prosa de prisa*, Vol I, op. cit. pp. 99-100.

[13] Ibid. pp. 5-6.

[14] Ibid. p. 7.

[15] Ibid. pp. 65-67.

[16] Ibid. p. 211.

[17] Ibid. pp. 298-299.

[18] Ibid. p. 81.

[19] Ibid. p. 80.

[20] Ibid p. 36.

[21] Ibid p. 8.

[22] In *Obra poética*, Vol. I. p. 114.

[23] *Prosa de prisa*, (Vol. I), pp. 206-211.

[24] Keith Ellis, "Conversation with Nicolás Guillén", *Jamaica Journal* Vol. 7, Nos. 1-2, 1973, p. 78. See also: *Recopilación de textos sobre Nicolás Guillén* - pp. 43-45.

[25] Ibid.

[26] Ibid.

[27] Sonia Aratán, "Entrevistas con Aimé Césaire", *CASA DE LAS AMERICAS*, No. 49, 1968, pp. 134-135.

[28] *Recopilación de textos*...op. cit. p. 44.

[29] René Depestre, "Problems of Identity for the Black Man in the Caribbean", CARIBBEAN QUARTERLY, Vol. 19, No. 3, Sept. 1973, p. 57.

[30] Ibid. (Spanish version in *CASA de las Américas*, No. 53, marzo-abril, 1969, pp. 19-28).

[31] "Entrevistas con Césaire", op. cit. p. 139.

[32] G.R. Coulthard, "Negritude - Reality and Mystification" *CARIBBEAN STUDIES*, Vol. 10., No. 1, 1970 pp. 42-51.

[33] *Recopilación de textos...*, op. cit. p. 43.

CHAPTER SEVEN

POETIC VARIATIONS ON A SINGLE THEME

Numerous commentators on the poetry Nicolás Guillén have been quick to acknowledge his perceptive interpretation of the mulatto experience in Cuba as a real and symbolic representation of the racial and cultural fusion that has resulted from the historical juxtaposition and interaction of peoples of African and European origins. Few, however, have attempted to examine, in detail, the poetic means by which Guillén enunciates and elaborates his central themes. Criticism has tended, generally to be more thematic and ideological than methodological, underscoring the African inheritance, the folkloric and nationalistic content, the uniqueness of the Afro-Hispanic amalgam, the social and cultural dimensions and the universal relevance.

As one step in an alternate direction, this chapter accepts the premise that the poet develops the theme of racial synthesis as a therapeutic measure for social and cultural rehabilitation in his society, but goes beyond that, aiming at investigating some strategies used in a selection of eight poems[1] to explore that single theme and demonstrate the fertility and diversity of devices utilized by the poet.

The major variations used in this selection are based on the poet's emotional and intellectual responses to his history, his keen sense of drama, his sensitive and shifting lines of approach, his exploitation of the unlimited possibilities of language for statement and suggestion, the rich texture and range of his imagery, his versification and poetic technique.

Guillén stands in the centre of two strong poetic currents: on the one hand the Hispanic tradition of popular and sophisticated verse forms cultivated over a time span of several centuries and enriched by the daring experiments of the Modernists;

and on the other hand, a rich oral tradition of popular folkloric forms imbued with the vitality, variety and verve of a people strùggling in the throes of "underdevelopment".

All the resources of the past and present are therefore available to him for the weaving of a new and varied fabric unrestricted by the demands of conformity, so that each poem emerges with an identity of its own while they all still bear a common and unique fourteen-letter stamp, the stamp of the author, "Nicolás Guillén".

FORMS

The wide range of poetic forms and techniques in this limited selection embraces the rigid and accomplished sonnet at one end and the novel and unexplored folk song at the other, with such intermediate models as the elegy, the ballad, the madrigal, the *canción* and free verse falling into place within the scale. No two poems are given the same form or technical structuring, so that at each turn there is a crafty manoeuvre that always takes the reader by surprise. This is the craft of a poet who is versed in Spanish metric forms and who has been influenced by the daring experimental and innovative artifices of the Modernists, but whose dreams of attainment and fulfillment have not led him away from the earth-bound realities of the folk.

His is an art devoid of excesses, yet untrammeled by conventionality. His modulations are but deliberate ways of heightening the exquisite, technical finesse that he brings to bear even on a form like the sonnet that is regarded as the acid test of poetic technique. It is the balance that he establishes between freedom and restraint that provides a possible keynote to his resounding success.

In the poem, "El abuelo" the poet uses the basic form of the Petrarchan sonnet cultivated in Spanish poetry since Boscán and Garcilaso de la Vega, but even here where he is faced with a highly specialized and often inflexible poetic form, the poet inserts his own innovative variations. Whereas the traditional Spanish form has generally adhered to a set rhyme pattern for the octet (ABBA, ABBA) while allowing a variety of combinations for the sextet (CDE, CDE; CDE, EDC; CDE, DEC; CDE, DCE; CDC, DCD), Guillén, in Modernist style, breaks loose from a tradition built up since the Renaissance and offers this daring combination - ABBA, CDDC, EFE, CFG -, a feat which aptly illustrates his unwillingness to be circumscribed or fettered by mere conventionality.

Besides, as if that were not enough, he sets aside the Italian hendecasyllable and demonstrates a characteristic Spanish penchant for even numbers by using the Alexandrine with its fourteen syllables as an alternate means of retaining the elevated and elegant quality of the sonnet. Then by shifting around his accents from line to line or from hemistich to hemistich he creates polyrhythmic effects in his varied combinations of dactyls and trochees.[2] The poem starts out with a mixed alexandrine carrying accents on the first and sixth syllables in each hemistich. The next two verses are similar in their combination of trochees and dactyls carrying their accents on the second, fourth and sixth and the third and sixth syllables, whilst the final verse of that first stanza remains strictly trochaic with accents on the second, fourth and sixth syllables of each hemistich. This medley of mixed, trochaic and dactylic verses is sustained throughout the poem, reinforced by variations in the use of anacrusis of one or two or even three syllables in some cases.

This is further enriched by the rhythm and harmony of his blending of vowel sounds. In "Esta mujer angélica de ojos septentrionales" for example, the dominant "e" sound of the first three words is deftly supported by the lighter, unaccented repetition of the same vowel sound in the next hemistich, and remains prominent in the rest of the stanza either at the end of lines in "europa" and "golpea" or interposed between two other accented vowels as in "vive atenta al ritmo" (i-e-i) or "ignora que en lo hondo" (o-e-o). That is why the isolated case of internal rhyme between "angélica" and "europa" is no accident. It is a vital part of the musical texture of the stanza.

This musicality is given greater diversification in the poet's manipulation of enjambement, pauses, caesura and hiatus. Each stanza has at least one case of enjambement - three of them used at the end of lines to give strength to the images they embrace (drumming, whiteness and bank of a stream) and the fourth appearing in the third stanza as one of the poet's bold Modernist attempts at an internal link between hemistiches (...Mírate las venas misteriosas).[3] In addition, the effective use of the pause between hemistiches in stanza one and in some subsequent verses (five, seven, eight, ten, thirteen and fourteen) provides a vital rhythmic dimension to the total musical effect. He achieves this rest through repeated use of qualifying phrases introduced by the preposition "de" or by separating a noun, phrase or a noun clause from the governing verb (lines seven, ten and fourteen) without destroying the smooth flow of the language or the meaning of the verse as a whole. Similar use is made of caesura, especially in lines six, eight and nine where logical rests marked by commas or exclamation marks do not adversely affect the metric rhythm of the verse. And, moreover, the deliberate hiatus of "europea", "golpea" and "lo hondo" in lines two and three, and "que huye" in line thirteen contributes to the overall rhythmic variety of a well ordered sonnet.

Other traditional forms are equally well manipulated to establish a close link between form and content. The elegy, for example, which dates back to the classical tradition, has been adapted to suit Guillén's own style and purposes. The solemn brooding of the elegy with its serious meditation is brought to bear on a family "tragedy" that is no less intense than the tragic death of the fourteen-year-old American student, Emmett Till, or the great Haitian Negro poet, Jacques Roumain, or the outstanding Cuban Negro trade unionist, Jesús Menéndez to whom he dedicates other elegies.

"El apellido", written in free verse, has an irregular structure representing an elaborate repertoire of verse forms - bi syllabic, tri-syllabic and tetra-syllabic verses interspersed between more familiar penta-syllabic, hepta-syllabic, nona-syllabic and hendeca-syllabic verses with the occasional insertion of a verse of thirteen, fourteen, fifteen or even sixteen syllables. This apparent formal looseness is but one way of taking advantage of the metric possibilities of the elegy and of dramatizing the experience of confusion and perplexity that the poet seeks to evoke out of the uncertainty of a name. Here the poet is obviously not relying primarily on any set form, rhyme or metric regularity for effect. The dramatic development of ideas, the forcefulness of telluric images, the use of rhetorical devices, and a fundamental rhythmic quality based on the predominance of the trochee, are appropriate devices that serve a clearer poetic interest in this poem. The poet starts out on a strong lyrical note meditating on a personal dilemma which he soon develops into a subject of public concern. The kind of identification he is pursuing transcends mere family connections, so that the poem is made to move away from the individualism of the early verses towards a collective, mystical resolution that borders closely on a kind of sublimation. This movement or development is not dependent on fixed stanzaic structures or any formal uniformity. The exploration of this particular state of mind and the resolution of this emotional problem seem to require a freer hand.

The madrigal also has a long tradition that is perhaps as old as the pastoral stream of the classical tradition, but Guillén transforms it into an instrument for dealing with sensual, urban themes drawn from among the simple black folk. "Puente" therefore falls into the same vein as the other madrigals in *Songoro Cosongo* or *West Indies Ltd.* - a brief, schematic form used to provide the pithy effect of a succinct comment on the sensuality of the coloured woman. This particular poem, however goes a little further than merely hinting at promiscuity. Its bare and crisp style encompasses suggestions of the role of the mulatto woman as a link in a society with two strong racial currents. The advantage of this form is that the subject matter is stripped down to its bare essentials, without losing any of the suggestiveness and musicality of poetry.[4]

From within the Hispanic tradition itself, Guillén utilizes the "balada" and the "canción" but not without adding his personal touch. In "Balada de los dos abuelos" he adheres to a basic octosyllabic pattern but is daring enough to break that pattern to create his own effects. First, he borrows the "estribillo" from the *villancico* tradition and establishes the theme of dual heritage. Then he moves on to what could be a stanza in a conventional Spanish "romance" with unrhymed first and third lines ("hueso" and "ancho") and normal second and fourth lines rhymed in assonance ("madera" and "guerra"). However, in order to reinforce, or perhaps clarify, the duality introduced in the "estribillo", he inserts two penta-syllabic lines which serve two functions: they break the euphony of the suave octo-syllables and therefore stand out as clear points of emphasis; and they introduce an unusual rhyme (between "hueso" and "negro" and between "ancho" and "blanco") that once more startles the reader.

This intermittent use of the pentasyllable along with the trisyllabic verses - "Me muero!" and "Me canso!" - serves to heighten the drama of the two grandfathers interacting in the poet's consciousness as well as on the historical and cultural planes. When these devices are moulded together with parentheses, exclamations, repetitions, parallelisms, the reintroduction of the "estribillo", and the progressive reduction of the metric structure from octosyllabic to hexasyllabic, then to quadrisyllabic, verse and a final bisyllabic word, "cantan", the net result is no longer a pure traditional Spanish ballad, but a new and characteristic Guillenian product.

The treatment of the "canción" is no less innovative. In "Canción del bongó (the version in *Antología Mayor*), Guillén adeptly side-steps the Italianate tradition with its variable combination of hendecasyllables and heptasyllables and sets up a uniform octosyllabic structure more in the tradition of the "villancico" or the "canción paralelística" popularised by Gil Vicente. This option opens up scope for the use of the "estribillo" which he skilfully weaves into the fabric of a fourteen-line stanzaic structure that carries a firm masculine rhyme on the oxytonic "o" of alternate lines producing a single, dominant, but unifying assonance throughout the poem.

Moreover, this "estribillo" which is fitted so compactly into the beginning and ending of the first stanza is made to appear only at the end of the second stanza, thus providing an alternate emphasis from the duplication used in the first stanza. But when one is expecting the poet to include the entire "estribillo" in the third stanza where he is making his concluding challenges, he surprises the reader by omitting it and leaving as a mild reminder of "aquí el que más fino sea" just a few suggestive words: "que aquí el mas alto soy yo".[5]

The use of octosyllabic verses here in place of the highly stylised hendecasyllable serves to retain a popular note reminiscent of the traditional "romance". That popular element is useful for underpinning the satirical intentions of the poet in his triangular approach to the theme. The effect achieved is that of the symbolic drum making a threefold popular attack on society, race and class using the three-stanza structure as the format. Finally, to place this popular social commentary in its proper Cuban context, Guillén reverts to the style of the "son" to produce the climax of the last stanza. The problem of racial prejudice is resolved and the people, all the people, can now dance together to the dominant sound of the bongo drum which in its own physical structure appropriately symbolises duality and unity.

From the rigid classiscal and traditionally established structures, Guillén moves to the less formal modes of free verse and folk song. “Dos niños” has as its only semblance of formality a stanzaic structure of six, five, five and six lines followed by an unrhymed couplet that repeats the first two lines of the poem. His combination of lines of seven, eleven, thirteen, fifteen, seventeen, eight, ten, fourteen, sixteen and even eighteen syllables could no doubt be regarded as a travesty. This deliberate formlessness along with his disregard for rhyme in a language that is so rich in its potential for assonance must therefore have some justification. The answer seems to rest in the question of the position from which the poet chooses to deal with his basic theme in this particular poem. The misery, the inelegance and squalor of the dog-like experience he conjures up would seem incongruous with the formal dress of strict metric patterns and contrived rhyme. The looseness of free verse adds to the sense of immediacy and directness that would seem appropriate and essential to the drama of suffering.

Now, if the test of Guillén's poetic technique lies in his mastery of the sonnet, the ballad, the madrigal, the elegy and the “canción”, then the measure of his originality is his imaginative and sensitive adaptation of the popular “son”. The poet, here, is dealing with a mode of expression that is flexible and capable of adaptation and variety. The “son” which emerged out of Oriente province is not always the same as the “son” that reaches the poor urban dweller of Havana, and is seldom the version played in night clubs and bourgeois ballrooms.[6] Neither is it the “son” from Guillén's typewriter.

Guillén himself has made it clear that he is not composing for popular folk groups (sextets) that specialise in performing the “son”.[7] His intention then is not to write words which get lost in the heat and frenzy of a dance hall, even though they capture the spirit of a popular song and dance. They are poems intended to stand by themselves on the written page, to be read, quietly or aloud, and appreciated for their poetic inspiration and poetic technique. But they are poems based in a particular form and created out of the conviction that that form is adequate for providing a structure and method which would capture the vitality and originality of the national spirit and national experience. His “son” is therefore a cultivated literary form distinct from the Spanish "romance" but also different from the rustic "son". While remaining sensitive to the rhythm and movements of the popular dance as well as the basic structures canonised by popular acceptance, Guillén has brought to this new poetry his own style, inventiveness, taste and awareness of the evocative power of the word. In his own words, it is a combination of an “ingenuity of technique which I have never had and a freshness of motivation which was necessary for them (the poems)”.[8] In fact, musicians inside and outside of Cuba have dared to put music to many of his poems - cantatas, arrangements for voice and piano, symphonies, etc., but the printed “son-poem” has continued to hold its own as a unique art form. Some essential features of this autochthonous form embraced and adapted to poetry by Guillén are:[9]

(i.) a two-part structure used in Oriente Province - a duet and a chorus with the latter serving as a reply to or a comment on the former;

(ii.) a thematic schema based on the "motivo" or statement of theme, the "letra" or development of the theme and the "montuno" which is a malicious or jesting comment;

(iii.) use of the "estribillo" - two, three or four lines used as an introduction and repeated throughout the song or poem in a variety of ways;

(iv.) repetition of phrases and ideas;

(v.) use of short, crisp exclamation such as "sí señor", "cómo no", "bien", "ay", "te digo", "amigo", for special rhythmic and emotional effects;

(vi.) the use of simple and popular speech forms, including the vernacular and reinforced by onomatopoeia and his highly rhythmic jitanjáforas;

(vii.) the strident sound and lively rhythm of the "tres" - a three-stringed musical instrument similar, in its effect, to the sound of the "cuatro";

(viii.) the syncopated rhythms of percussion instruments;

(ix.) a lively rhythm at the end, which bursts out into excited laughter and dancing;

(x.) a tendency to forget the initial issue or problem

when one gets carried away in the excitement of the
ending; or rather, a tendency to resolve problems
in the ecstasy of song and dance.

"Son número 6" aptly illustrates most of the principal aspects of the "son". The poetic persona who plays the role of singer or narrator engages in an interesting interplay with his audience who serve as a chorus. The riddle he uses to initiate his story, the three-part development of his statement - beginning, expansion, ending -, the use of the "estribillo" (Yoruba soy, soy-lucumí/mandinga, congo, carabali)[10] in all its variations, the invitation to dance in the middle of the poem and the final resolution of the narrative in the frenzy of an endless song and dance, are ways of capturing some of the drama of the actual "son".

THE DRAMATIC APPROACH

The "son" then is one of various vehicles through which the poet can explore a single theme; but this varied technical approach is only one of the several ways in which Guillén opens up for himself a wide berth for viewing and reworking his material. One line of approach is to develop a variety of dramatic poetic modes that bring the poems to life. His use of a dramatic opening for each of the poems in question always proves arresting and different and sets a firm base for a drama that is always well sustained throughout the poem itself.

The use of the ghost image in "Balada de los dos abuelos" introduces the theme with an eeriness that haunts the reader and the persona alike from the introductory couplet straight through to the end of the poem where the ghosts are shouting, dreaming, weeping and singing in one's memory. There is no respite for poet nor reader in this drama of taunts that one lives daily. To read the poem is also to relive that drama of the sub-conscious which is so essential a reality in the totality of the individual's experience.

The sound of the drum in "Canción del bongó" is a challenging call to order, a dramatic and unavoidable summons to consciousness, a compelling voice that penetrates to the heart, mocks the pretentious, condemns violence and hatred and establishes itself triumphantly as a unifying agent towering above all petty differences and prejudices. The image of the singing drum is not unusual but provocatively dramatised here as a persona knocking at the door. It is like a stage act where the drum is the protagonist teasing, cajoling, mocking and persuading. It is an act from which the reader cannot be detached; in fact, he is not even allowed to hesitate or say "Just a minute", "Coming now". He is caught up by the drum image transplanted fully into the poetic world of the drum where disunity, disharmony, duplicity and meanness are being expunged.

The firm and confident start of "Son número 6" gives a strong impression of a militant pro-African identification; and there is nothing in the first four stanzas to negate this black image of the persona. It seems like a deliberate move by the poet to attack from a one-sided position, adopting a deceptive racial line before he suddenly and dramatically turns around to face the issue squarely in the middle of the field, only to conclude that the one-sided position is untenable. The line "Estamos juntos desde muy lejos"[11] is the dramatic turning point in centre-field, the eye opener, the vital clue to a proper understanding of the real import of the poem.

"El abuelo" starts with an ironic statement of a problem of ignorance and lop-sided thinking underscored by the dichotomy: white-black, skin-veins; appearance-reality; ignorance-knowledge. The resolution of the initial problem leaves the irony even more firmly embedded in the reader's mind, for the "angelic, nordic woman" is dramatically confronted by the ghost of the black grandfather who was responsible for the curly hair on her white forehead but whom she had ignored all along.

"Puente" begins with a striking but uncomplicated image that gives away no emotion and which, contrary to the view of Alberto Lamar Schweyer, shows no sign of recrimination.[12] It is terse, perhaps even cold; highly suggestive in the first two lines, both factual and suggestive in the next two and suddenly becomes cryptic towards the end; a successful dramatic exercise in the use of concise forms.

"El Apellido" however, opens with a sober but provoking reference to childhood reinforced by an image of new birth; but what seems like a smooth surface is suddenly rippled by an arousing image of a password to the stars. This sets the drama in motion, unleaching highly lyrical responses - (passion, protest, anguish) which eventually dissolve into the abstraction of images of air and liberty. The approach here is attempting to resolve a personal problem of identity through a series of rhetorical questions, sighs, exclamations, repetitions and cynical remarks, or by word play touched with irony and perplexity. It shows an interesting combination of deep emotionality and analytical rationality in the face of this historical, cultural and geneological tragedy with which the poet is preoccupied.

"Dos niños" is the only one of these poems that strikes at the question of duality from the first word. Others approach it inversely, indirectly, obliquely, except for "Balada de los abuelos" which approaches the issue on a direct line, though with an element of suspense. However, from that first line of "Dos niños" there is a dramatic and unrelenting hammering of the idea of duality until it leaves a resounding echo in the reader's consciousness - two children, two branches, two beggars, two dogs, two heads, two pairs of bare feet, two mouths, two hands, two stomachs, untied; one black and the other white.

POWER OF IMAGERY

This ear for the dramatic is blended with a keen eye for the pictorial and for natural linkages, and a strong passion for unity and harmony. This represents an essential dimension of the substance of Guillén's images. One sees, feels, hears, smells and tastes what the poet perceives and offers, and senses the intangible goals he pursues, for the texture of his imagery is such that it always draws the reader into an experience of truth as the poet has perceived it imaginatively.

The telluric imagery of "El apellido" seems to be a deliberate means of defining identity in the pristine terms of one's connections with all nature and also a means of stressing the fundamental importance of an awareness of one's origins to a clear understanding of the totality of one's experience. When the poet perceives his ancestral heritage as " a geography full of dark mountains, deep and bitter valleys, abysses, subterranean galleries with great moist stones, islands jutting out of black pools and a pure stream of ancient waters falling from a proud heart with a fresh, deep sound in a place full of burning trees", he is evidently striving to capture not only the intimacy and vitality of a connection with a natural source of which he sees himself as a direct product, but also the drama of a history that robs him of that connection. He is also penetrating beneath surface reality into the depths of the subconscious and into a realm of supersensory perceptions that take one back to what he calls "the roots of my roots", by way of dreams, sensations and visions. From here, however, he seems to move on to make the point that it is these elemental connections that lead man away from individualism and egocentricity into a deeper collective consciousness that diminishes the importance of blood connections and transforms that "navigable blood" of the first stanza into the "combative blood" of the last stanza. It is no longer a question of mere consubstantiality, but of solidarity expressed in forceful elemental images.

The image of the woman-bride straddling two worlds in "Puente" is surprising enough to capture the alert reader's attention and realistic enough not to border on the absurd. Then when those worlds are specified in terms of actual dwelling places we are taken even nearer to the truth of the proximity and intimacy out of which that mulatto woman-bridge must have been formed. The image draws together very definite racial, social and historical associations in that single arresting picture. The black-white combination are all part and parcel of the poetic intent.

Similarly, the child-branch picture of "Dos niños" engages one in a sensuous response as well as a sensory experience in the attempt to imagine the sap being fed into the branches from the stem. As a first surprise, one soon realises that that sap which should be the life-giving substance, is in fact, nothing but an unpalatable juice of misery. This initial image is then extended and intensified through another parallel image of hungry dogs feeding on an unsavoury dish, and then dramatised through graphic pictorial scenes of barefooted, mendicant children full of pustules and lice. All five senses are taxed here and through them one is made to recognise close affinities between the poetic world and the real world. This dramatisation is intended to underscore the poet's passion for the unity and solidarity so well captured in his return, in the final lines, to the concrete image of two branches solidly established in the tree trunk.

The ghost image of the grandfathers in "Balada de los abuelos" is forceful for its sensuousness and evocative power:

> Sombras que sólo yo veo,
> me escoltan mis dos abuelos.[13]

The shadows, though inconcrete, have a poetic substantiality in their context, an impelling presence that is both visualised and felt. In this way, one is brought face to face with an inescapable truth about one's heredity; one is led by, or perhaps trapped between, two escorts, two guides to destiny and the fact that they are ghosts makes the image even more portentous.

Equally engrossing and encompassing is the powerful river image contained in the riddle of "Son Número 6". The purely sensuous value of the image is intensified by the dramatic function of the riddle. For a moment one wonders if the solution to the riddle must be found in solidarity among Yoruba descendants only, especially when the stanza commencing with: "La ceiba ceiba con su penacho"[14] seems to be suggesting that every man must be true to himself and identify with his own. Whose blood is involved? Pure Yoruba blood? The riddle leaves the reader puzzled. The real import of the river image is dramatically suspended and the reader held at bay until the poet unveils his clues in "Estamos juntos desde muy lejos/ jóvenos, viejos/negros y blancos, todo mezclado."[15]

The effectiveness of Guillén's imagery is, in great measure, explained by the element of surprise in the dramatic correspondences he creates. Such correspondences are not only seen in the making of the single image but also in the contextural connections between different images. The bridge might establish the idea of a link, a mere point of contact, and would therefore be inadequate to convey the idea of genetic synthesis. The bridge is just an overpass beneath which another image - the river of blood - must be created to produce a sense of completeness. "Puente" therefore needs "Son número 6" as its logical complement both for its historical perspective and its emphasis on fusion.

Similarly, "Canción del bongó", effective as it is by itself, deals with the theme only from the angle of social contact or social and historical interaction. It therefore needs "El abuelo" to provide a complementary image that can go deeper into the concept of ethnic admixture; hence the strange image of the rhythm of her European blood played by a Negro.

THE CONTROLLED APPROACH

Taken in isolation or together, Guillén's images tend to appear as living events or dynamic pictures of a poetic experience transmitted as a genuine discovery of some truth about humanity. This discovery of truth is made through a combination of emotional and intellectual responses to a national historical experience. There is a conscious effort to place the whole question of race and identity in historical perspective in order to avoid emotional excesses and to create a sense of balance and wholeness where the temptation to engage in vituperation and divisiveness is great.

The early poem, "Ayé me dijeron negro"[16] is one in which the persona comes closest to recrimination, but finds a moderately controlled answer in the accuser's family history. The black man, provoked by a light-skinned mulatto, feels compelled to combat the treatment of contempt he receives with a caustic and almost cruel retort reminding the mulatto of a geneological fact[17] he has either consciously or unconsciously ignored:

> You t'ink you white
> but ah know who you gran mudder is.
> Drag she out o' de kitchen,
> drag she out:
> dat Mooma Inés!

This kind of retaliation is eschewed in later poems such as "El abuelo" where the poet chooses an interestingly objective and detached stance to deal with a similar problem of superiority complexes and hidden prejudices. What Guillén has done is to clothe his attack on racial prejudices in the subtle suggestion that nature and history have done their irreparable work in the bloodstream and that that work cannot be altered by prejudice, ignorance, or false appearances. He stands aside to chuckle rather than get angry, to smile rather than frown. In fact, this attitude comes through very effectively in the satirical tones of "La canción del bongó". When the poet withdraws, he allows the drum-persona to engage in a kind of raillery with the "brown-skinned and dark-souled types who owe their shades more to their blood than to the sun", those for whom it has grown dark on the inside even when night has not fallen on the outside".

This tendency towards an objective focus can readily be recognised in those poems in which there is an overt attempt to explain and resolve the dilemma in terms of pre-colonial history, the middle passage, slavery and the post-emancipation reality. In "El apellido" one sees clear evidence of the possibilities for invective, bitterness and anger as the poet painfully goes through his anguished musings on his family history, his sense of loss, his quest for his hidden name and the tragedy of the Middle Passage which he calls the "enigma of the waters". Nevertheless, the personal dilemma is sublimated in the wider experience of human suffering seen in its historical context as a call to solidarity and struggle for the liberation of man and of the spirit.

Guillén's answer to the historical problem seems simple: the facts of interracial cohabitation, slavery and exploitation, the tragedy of the Middle Passage and their concomitant dispossession, alienation and discrimination, must be acknowledged and overcome by the fusion of the strength, the fighting spirit, the dreams and hopes, (in short, the positive dimensions) of the dual heritages of equally dynamic currents:

> Both raise their strong heads;
> Both of equal size,
> shout, dream, weep, sing.
> Dream, weep, sing.
> Weep, sing.
> Sing![18]

Undoubtedly, the message of the "mulatto" character of the national identity can be summarised crudely in a line or a sentence or even in extended prose. The object of the poetic exercise must therefore be to explore as many creative avenues for coming to terms with a delicate and sensitive issue that is a source of inspiration and challenge to a people involved in defining their own vision of themselves and their destiny. Cuba's national poet has paved the way for that kind of imaginative search for insights and that inventive effort to communicate sensitively by using all the creative resources of the past to enrich the experience of the future. This is an essential part of his understanding of the revolutionary meaning of culture.

NOTES

1. (a) "Canción del bongó", (b) "Balada de los dos abuelos", (c) "El abuelo", (d) "Dos niños", (e) "Son número 6", (f) "El apellido", (g) "Puente", (h) "Ayé me dijeron negro". See Guillén, *Obra poetica.* (Vol. I), op. cit., pp. 116, 137, 149, 152, 231, 394, for (a) - (f); See Appendix II, Chapter Seven, Notes 4 and 16 for (g) and (h).

2. See T. Navarro Tomás, *Arte del verso,* Mexico, 1959, pp. 22-23.

3. "...Look at your mysterious veins."

4. "Puente" (from *Songoro Cosongo: poemas mulatos,* La Habana, ed. Imp. Ucar García y Cía, 1931 p. 22; Reproduced by Alberto Lamar Schweyer in "La musa mulata" *Recopilación de textos sobre Nicolás Guillén* (CASA), \ p. 257.

5. "he who thinks he is the best here"; "here, I am the highest of all."

6. Compare: Ramón Vasconcelos, "Motivos de son" in *Recopilación de textos sobre Nicolás Guillén,* op. cit., p. 244.

7. Nicolás Guillén, *Prosa de prisa,* Vol. I., op. cit., p. 20. See also Angel Augier, "La raíz cubana" in *Recopilación de textos sobre Nicolás Guillén,* p. 143.

8. Ibid. p. 21.

9. See: *Recopilación de textos sobre Nicolás Guillén,* pp. 84-85; 147-149; 152-154; 180-182; 244-245; 248-249.

10. "I am yoruba, I am lucumí mandinga, congo, carabalí.

11. "We have been together from long ago"

12. Ibid. p. 257.

13. Shadows which I alone see
My two grandfathers escorting me.

14. "Let the ceiba be a ceiba with its crest"

15. "We have been together from long ago
young, old
blacks and whites, all mixed."

16. Ibid, p. 209. (From *Motivos de son*, La Habana, ed. Imp. Papelería de Rambia, Bonza y Cía., 1930, p. 9. Reproduced in: Angel Augier, *Nicolás Guillén, notas para un estudio biográfico-crítico*, La Habana, 1962, Tomo I, p. 126. See Appendix II for text of poem.

17. The use of grandparents in Guillén's poetry is often symbolic, a mere geneological point of reference. In his personal case, e.g. it was his great-grandfathers who were white and black, not his grandparents.

18. "Balada de los dos abuelos" (*Obra poética*...Vol. I, p. 139).

CHAPTER EIGHT

THE SATIRICAL MODE

The cutting edge of Guillén's poetry is his widely varied use of satire. He can be mild and teasing at times, or tauntingly humorous and sardonic at other times, or he can become aggressively caustic and wounding, particularly in his political satires. His mood, like his mode, changes constantly from a position of critical and sympathetic understanding, through various stages of frowning, wry laughter and controlled anger, to a level of critical severity that borders on acrimony and rage.

His early protest poetry represents some of his milder satirical modes. *Motivos de son* and *Sóngoro Cosongo* illustrate the use of playful humor to underscore some of the truths and horrors of the social order and some inconsisencies and anomalies in social attitudes. "Negro bembón", "Mulata", "Puente", "Mi Chiquita", and "La canción del bongó" deal critically with the questions of racial prejudice and social discrimination, but without the venom and opprobrium of angry protest. Similarly the social protest of these two early volumes is veiled in irony rather than virulence; the message is more often implied than stated.

Some of this gentle satirical form is carried forward to his later poetry as a means of dealing with misguided types who are unaware of the full implications of their counter-revolutionary attitudes. Poems such as "¿Puedes?", "Responde tú...", and "Ay, qué tristeza que tengo!" from *Tengo*, or "La herencia" from *La reuda dentada* recapture that understanding tone but are no less critical and incisive for their control and gentleness. The rhetorical devices used by the poet are characteristically humane ways of cushioning the force of his penetrative satire.

A similar streak can be observed in his satirical use of English words and phrases. It is clear that he recognizes and is critical of the cultural, political, social and economic implications of the U.S. presence in the Caribbean and the symbolic role of their language as an instrument of imperialism. This comes out very plainly in "West Indies Ltd." or "Elegía a Jesús Menédez" where the satire is biting and harsh, but it is used more subtly in poems such as "Tú no sabe inglé", "Canción puertorriqueña", "Ciudades", and "Problemas del subdesarrollo". The first of these four poems strikes an early blow at the subservient psychology of an imitative English, "the English of four-footed cicerones" with their superficial tourist gimmicks; the second deals with the cultural confusion caused by an imposed duality brought about by imperialist invasion; the third looks critically at the political dilemma of British colonies in the Caribbean which still chant "God save the King", and relates it to the irony of the Panamanian situation with its dominant U.S. presence; the last poem deals with questions of culture and identity and underlines the important role of language in the definition and understanding of these two concepts. In all of these contexts language is seen as a tool that the imperialists can use for their own end, but which the poet can also manipulate for his own satirical purposes.

This tongue-in-cheek manner of Guillén sometimes takes the form of wry humor achieved through punning, or the use of derisive or of fanciful sobriquets. In the political satires of 1949,[1] political figures are identified by nicknames and distorted versions of their political roles: President Carlos Prio Socarrás becomes "el Pitcher Nacional", an incompetent baseball player (p. 275); ex-President Ramón Grau San Martin is referred to variously as "Mongo", a thief hanging on a cross (p. 277), as "Professor Al Capone", the American gangster (p. 283), as "Galimatías". the confused orator (p. 283), or as Mongo Galimatías", the charlatan (p. 289); the Minister of Agriculture, Francisco Grau Alsina is a yam ("el ñame de agricultura") being dug up by a crane, (*Grau* being uprooted by a *grúa*, pp. 281, 282).

The pun seems relatively mild when compared with his more contemptuous treatment of crooked political figures. The "Premier", Antonio de Varona, is offered a pistol as a prize ("premio") for his pretentious "law against gansterism" in spite of the Government's own complicity with the armed gangs (pp. 272, 541). Elsewhere, he uses the euphemistic "hijo de yuca" to replace "hijo de puta" or "hijo de perra" ("son-of-a-cassava" for "son-of-a-bitch"), but the satirical undertones are clear especially when used in reference to "his Excellency Carlos Prio Socarrás" (p. 286) or President Harry Truman (p. 290).

This direct attack on personalities is an aggressive satirical vein that characterises his journalism of the period 1949-53.[2] It goes beyond the sardonic element in "West Indies Ltd." (Section I) where the poet "laughs" at some of the tragic aspects of West Indian life and West Indian personalities: poverty in the midst of wealth and prosperity; the drying up of brains and flowers alike in the tropical heat; the symbolic loin cloth beneath the ostentatious décor; the vain display of politicians, orators, political parties, banks, bankers, lawyers, journalists, doctors, stockbrokers and legislators; insularity and narrowness; the image of the tourist's haven; false notions of nobility and aristocratic identity; the folly of imitativeness, vain aspirations and false ambition.

The new thrust is the output of a fearless poet-journalist who deliberately confronts the political outrages of the time and openly denounces the repression, corruption and stagnation characteristic of dictatorships. He will lampoon Prío Socarrás, Grau San Martin, or Batista (pp. 275, 277, 319-321) for their legeerdemain without attempting to conceal their underground agents: the assassin of Jesús Menédez becomes "a jackal walking among men" (p. 289); the spineless Trade Unionist, Eusebio Mujol who does not even need the mask of an animal (p. 321); and the fat civil servant who has some god-father to protect him is like a "budget vampire" (p. 348).

This tendency towards caricature and the burlesque is one which recurs quite frequently throughout his poetry in his attacks on imperialism and fascism. The picture one gets of Mussolini in "Soldado en Abisinia" is the grotesque figure of a devil-pirate with long hands, bending friendishly over a map of Africa. In intention, that picture is not very different from the picture of Senator McCarthy in "Pequeña letanía grostesca en la muerte del senador McCarthy", where he is featured as Senator McMonkey, McVulture and McMare flanked, on his death-bed, by monkeys, vultures, mares and frogs.

It is rarely that Guillén's satire approaches the bitterness of acrimony or the abusiveness of opprobrium, but whenever it does, it is reserved for provocative acts of aggression and disrespect on the part of imperialist powers. He can choose simply to turn to ridicule and mockery in "Futuro" (*Poemas de transición*) when he wishes to expose the folly of U.S. military intervention; or in "Caña" he can can adopt the role of the cartoonist and delineate just the bare, basic features of U.S. economic domination and exploitation; or he can opt for th controlled cynicicm of some of his folk characters - singers, maracas player, guitarrist etc. But he can also assume the envenomed outbursts of Dario's diatribe in his anti-U.S. poems, "Los cisnes" and "A Roosevelt" or the reproachful and angry protest of Neruda in his *Canto general* or his "testamento poético".

Guillén's poems, "Perro Yanqui" and "Venganza" in Volume I, or "Marines U.S.A." and "Frente al Oxford" in Volume II are poems born out of "sacred rancour" against "shameless yankees" like Johnson, Lynch, Walker, Truman, McCarthy, Al Capone and "the dirty, drunken marines who walk in shitty shoes" looking for prostitutes and pissing on the statue of Cuba's national hero, José Marti, in the Central Park in Havana. The tone here is highly vituperative and resembles the note of invective that can also be recognized in the poems, "U.S.A.", "Lo que faltaba" and "Little Rock" which deal with the racial question in the Southern States of the U.S.A. All of them reveal a deep sense of righteous indignation and justifiable revolt, which becomes more pronounced when Guillén chooses to contrast those indictable U.S. strategies with the virtues he sees in the Soviet Union, as in the poem "Union Soviética" in Volume II. There is an inherent danger in this kind of comparison, but fortunately, that idealistic presentation of the Soviet Union is not overplayed, so that even the outrage of these poems shows some balance and control.

The crowning success of Guillén's satire then has been his ability to work out a balanced blend of pungent political comment with a profound commitment to broad human concerns.

NOTES

1. Guillén, *Obra poética* (Vol. I), op. cit. pp. 269-299.
2. Ibid. pp. 299-356. See "Coplas de Juan Descalzo" etc.
3. Pablo Neruda, *Incitación al nixonicidio y alabanza de la revolución chilena*, Barcelona, 1973.

CHAPTER NINE

THE PRIVATE MUSE AND PERSONAL VOICE

The case of Nicolás Guillén typifies that of the committed Revolutionary poet who retains a private and personal voice. He can speak with a variety of public voices - popular troubadour, rural peasant, urban vagrant, anguished mother, disgruntled soldier, embittered Negro, and the collective "yo" of the masses -, but the individual voice of the poet is equally distinct when his personal Muse chooses to speak from within.

The two are not mutually exclusive. The poet who deals with the details and particularities of the Cuban experience knows how to transfer that experience onto a more general human plane on the basis of an ideological interpretation of broad human concerns. He is therefore able to translate the particular into the universal and the concrete into the abstract, by way of an interpretative extraction of ideological and transcendental meanings. Implicit in this, however, is the danger of becoming an ideological pedagogue on the one hand, or a pedant and doctrinaire on the other; but Guillén saves himself from both by his ability to distinguish between that public voice, with the full import of its moral judgments on society, and the personal voice whose Muse contemplates the themes of religion, art, love, death and destiny.

This idea of the alternate Muse surfaced early in his poetry in "La nueva musa" (1927):

> Before, the poet was a musician
> dancing about in front of his orchestra...
> Now, the poet goes deep within himself
> and from there, conducts his orchestra.[1]

Two years later, in the poem "Viaje interior" he speaks of a "projected voyage into himself" which, without stretching the poem too far, could be a journey through the realities of experience and on to the plane of the recondite and the transcendental:

> There must be many new things
> in me deep within my own oblivion.[2]

But it could also be a simple journey into the inner self that has an eye for earthy realities like nature, women and love.

NATURE:

Separate from any preoccupation with society and politics (though not always divorced from them), it is possible to perceive an underlying personal response to nature. Rivers, the sea, water, clouds and the sky do have their symbolic meanings in the context of the flow of experience, the continuum of time and the heights of human aspirations, dreams and hopefulness, but landscapes and seascapes are also there for the sheer message of forcefulness and energy they hold for the poet.

The treatment of the Caribbean landscape might have something to say about the shaping of a volatile and explosive Caribbean character and a Caribbean personality or the shaping of its "culture-scape" and about the vitality and exhuberance of the environment in which history has enacted so many dramatic scenes, but the evocation of the tropical landscape also has a beauty of its own that reveals the poet's deep personal attachment to nature in a way that is devoid of the superfluity of romantic sentimentality. It is a serious evocation of Caribbean contexts which inevitably help to define Caribbean man.

The poem, "Acana", conjures up a picture of the density of a forest without the use of descriptive excesses. The effect is achieved through the kind of simple rhythmic repetition that engraves a graphic picture on the mind of the reader/listener. "Ebano real" and "Palma sola" achieve similar effects, one by the suggestive evocation of hardness, durability and usefulness, and the other by the suggestive use of images of height, dreams, liberty and hunting that evoke the dominant and lofty presence of the palm tree. Like them, "Calor" conveys the intensity of heat of a tropical night through striking, penetrative images of the heat "cracking" the night which "falls roasted" over the river while "the islands go on sailing ablaze."[3] And "Palabras en el trópico" uses vivid, vigorous images of bursting energy and heat that remind one of the forceful telluric imagery of "El apellido" and "Llegada":

Tropics,
your hard bonfire
toasts the lofty clouds
and the deep sky girded by the Mid-day arc.
On the bark of trees you dry out
the anguish of the lizard.
You grease the wheels of the winds
to frighten the palm trees.
With a great red arrow
you traverse the heart of the forest
and the flesh of the rivers...

I see your crude hands
barbarously tear open the seeds
to snatch from them the opulent tree...[4]

"Elegía cubana", "Turiguanó" and "El negro mar" along with "Un largo lagarto verde" all look at Cuban and Caribbean sea-scape, admittedly in its historical context, but nonetheless with a keen eye for its natural physical qualities:

beaten by hard waves
and adorned with soft foam,
beneath the sun that oursues it
and the wind that rejects it...[5]

Inherent in this private response to the physial environment, however, is an underlying intellectual dimension. Sometimes, the landscape is made to reflect the history of the region and its contemporary social tensions; at other times, one perceives a sense of respect and even reverence for mother earth and related phenomena - space, sky, water, wind, rain - particularly when they are seen as symbols of the indomitable spirit of man or of the ascendancy of human rights and human dignity. The sovereignty of nature is upheld in "¿Puedes?" as an alternative concept to or antidote for, materialism, rapine and exploitation. The conclusion of the poem points not only towards that idea of the primacy of nature but, by inference, towards such concepts as the equality of all men, natural justice, and the undefined but undeniably real purviews of human capabilities. It is, to a large extent, this intellectual tendency towards abstraction which has saved the thematic content of Guillén's enormous *oeuvre* from sliding into the pedestrian groove of so many writers of protest literature, and for this, that private Muse with its deeply personal responses has to be given full credit.

DEATH:

Another important personal element has been his treatment of the theme of death. After an initial expression of disquiet in his early poem, "Rima triste", from *Cerebro y corazón* (1922), where death assumes the frightening and awesome threat of extinction, the poet progressively moves towards a more positive and almost millenarian view of death. He gives up the emotionalism of "Sonata crepuscular", "Nocturno", "Canción de los sauces", and "Canción de invierno", and the negativism of "De profundis", so that in the same collection, "La amarga ironía" rejects the idea of suicide at the same time that it rejects the notion of living in servility, submission or resignation to the injustices and rigours of life, and, by implication, therefore points towards confrontation and struggle. "Gota" takes up the same strain:

> It is not good enough for man to live
> perpetually surrounded
> by death, so that
> it is she who guides his footsteps
> and at the end he surrenders
> without even vain complaints...[6]

By 1945, "Iba yo por un camino" and "Pero que te pueda ver" face up to death with the full courage and maturity that experience brings. These two poems bring to the forefront an element of defiance which characterises this phase of the poet's life. The political activist having now matured ideologically, has clearly recognised that personal sacrifice is a part of the challenge of Revolutionary struggle. the fear of death and the sentimental weeping that accompanies death have evaporated and a pragmatic and stoical outlook have emerged. This attitude is humorously expressed in "Muerte" which appeared in *La paloma de vuelo popular* (958) where the poet awaits his final day with curiousity, and in readiness for the inevitable encounter. "Epigrama #1" in *La rueda dentada* (1972) crystallises this acceptance:

> Will I tell you that I am excited
> over a vast and powerful matter
> which no one before me has touched:
> My death.[7]

And "Sobre la muerte" puts on the final stamp, coming as it did during his dramatic encounter with death in 1971 when he suffered a serious heart attack. Here, the poet strips deathof all its mystery and terror and reduces it to the commonplace:

> Death can be called dagger-prone and bloodless Caesar,
> but it is also the lovely, decorative and throat-cut

pheasant
which died to preside over the promising joy of this
night. It is
the city dog drivelling its strychnine,
suffering in the streets surrounded by boys...
We eat death every day,
and death gnaws away at us every night.[8]

THE ELEGIAC OPTIMISM:

It is with this view of death in mind that one must examine Guillén's elegies from as early as his *Poemas de transición* (1926-1929) up to the death of Ernesto Che Guevarra (1967). Of these, one is dedicated to his poetic art ("Elegía moderna del motivo cursi"), one to Camagüey, his native city ("Elegía camagüeyana"), one to Cuba, his native land ("Elegía cubana"), two to his traumatic history ("El apellido" and "Por el camino del mar"), one to the tragedy of the West Indian political and economic experience ("West Indies Ltd."), two to popular folk characters ("Velorio de Papá Montero" and "Elegía a un soldado vivo"), one to his father ("Canción filial"), and the remaining seven to personalities as varied as Martín Dihigo, the distinguished Cuban baseball player and Guillén's friend; the Russian cosmonaut, Yuri Gagarin; the political leader, Ho Chi Mihn of Viet Nam, the innocent Negro youth, Emmett Till who fell vicitm to white racist opposition to integration in schools in the South of the United States; the Haitian writer, Jacques Roumain; the Cuban trade union leader, Jesús Menéndez and the Revolutionary hero, Che Guevara.

The prevailing theme in all of these elegies is the denial of the supremacy and finality of death. Images of life and hope constantly overcome the challenge of death as if the poet-optimist must draw moral embers from the ashes and cinders of death with its threat of confrontation, frustration and defeat. Without being overtly religious, the elegies convey the millenarian lyricism, confidence and optimism of St. Paul's outburst: "Death is swallowed up in victory. O death, where is thy sting? O grave, where is thy victory?"[9]

"Canción filial" refuses to accept the notion that death can deprive him of the wealth of experience and influence that is embodied in his father's image. The poet must discover a way of transcending the barriers of time, space, death and the lack of physical contact by rescuing the moral fibres and spiritual sinews of parental love and filial devotion:

Father: the one thing that's certain
is that you are not dead...

You, who do not sleep, watch over my little dream...

Keep me at your side as you did before,
Hide my faults, share in my joys...

Wrap me up in yourself, though I cannot see you...[10]

Similarly, he must rise above the negativism and destructiveness of historical evidence and find symbols of regeneration and new associations as a means of giving meaning to existence and struggle. The meanness and vileness of man's motivations and actions in the course of history can be extracted from the harsh memories of piracy, slavery. exile, oppression and moral and spiritual death in "Elegía" ("Por el camino de la mar/vino el pirata"); and the evils of dispossession and dislocation can be extracted from "El apellido". When the two are taken together, however, they lead to the conclusion that out of a *scenario* of destruction, a message of resurrection, collective survival and freedom can be gleaned:

What does it matter then...?
Come and see my name!
My unlimited name,
made out of innumerable names;
that name of mine, different,
free and my own, different and yours,
different and free as the air.[11]

It is this vision of liberty emerging out of scenes of death that inspires "Elegía a Emmett Till" where the poet denounces indifference in the face of the cruel death of a child and invokes the animated Mississippi to take a positive stand on the side of justice. Here the message is indirect and comes through symbols - "fists, birds, dreams and metals" -, symbols of strength, resistance and freedom; but it is clear. Nature itself comes alive when death takes on the ugly face of assassination, and so the human spirit is awakened and enlivened to resist the agents of death.

Out of this capacity for resistance, hope emerges as a constant factor alongside the Revolutionary heroism of personalities such as Che, Gagarin, Roumain and Menéndez. Whereas "Elegía Camagüeyana" suggests the improtance of hope as a vital aspect of the solidarity that leads out of darkness and into the fulfilment of dreams

Know that I speak to you and dream,
Know that I look for you in the middle of the night...

in the middle of the night and hope[12]

and "Elegía Cubana" maintains the living image of revolutionary heroes and the "pure fire" that symbolises their revolutionary heroism

Maceo sparkles in his safe zenith,
Martí lights his blue star above[13]

it is the individual cases of his personal friends and heroes that are used to highlight the counterpointing of sad themes and hopeful motifs. In the case of Gagarin's death, there is no need to weep over what seems like a tragedy, for death is swallowed up in the uproar of the accident. Images of a flowering branch, the resounding echo of a voice and a contemptuous smile represent the triumph of the hero over death:

His life
is not a buried rose
nor is it converted into mud or moss.
...The hero's life
is suspended from a star.
...his great resounding voice is distributed
from life to life and from life to life.[14]

A parallel note is struck in the case of Che Guevarra's death which becomes the signal for Revolutionary activity as an instrument for defeating death:

Not because you have fallen
is your light any less bright.
A horse of fire
bears your guerrilla sculpture
amongst the wind and clouds of the Sierra...

Wait for us. We will join you. We wish
to die so as to live as you died,
to live as you now live.[15]

....

Do not weep for this is not the time
for tears and handkerchief,
but for the machete in hand.[16]

In the elegies to Jacques Roumain and Jesús Menéndez images of rebirth, renovation, revival and fecundity are used to point to the optimism of the future that conquers death and the past:

But with every sigh a child is born.
Every day night gives birth to a yellow
and optimistic sun, that fertilises the wasteland...
The old lance flourishes planted.
Hope burns in our hands
Dawn is slow, but it's approaching[17]

....

A tree grew with blood from my wound.
A bird sings to life from it.
Tomorrow is announced with a trill.[18]

"Lectura de domingo" which draws a message from the Bolivian diary of Che Guevarra sees the issue of his death as a signal for explosion/conflagration and rebirth:

Afterwards silence.
There are no more pages.
The matter gets serious.
This thing has finished soon.
It finishes.
It will explode.
It dies out.
It will be born.[19]

And the paradoxical "Elegía a un soldado vivo" which deals specifically with the tragedy of exploitation, a kind of "death in life", also gives clear indications of the hope that should inspire rebellion and lead into a new and open future:

Ah beloved, beloved!
Not you dead soldier
you who are asleep.

Come and shout in my streets
You who are awake,
you, with tongue, teeth and ears...

for, so must the world see suspended
our open future...[20]

It is remarkable too that even Guillén's attempt to define his conception of art and its functionality is translated into elegiac terms in his "Elegía moderna del motivo cursi".[21] The poem marks the death of cheap and frivolous effusiveness and sentimentality and the birth of a strong, respectable and loving poetic expression that is grounded in reality. The art he pursues and the dreams he nurtures are inextricably interlocked in this process of renewal that characterises his personal vision of the world and of human experience.

RELIGION:

The theme of religion shows an interesting development from the faith and simplicity of adolescence to the cynicism and critical outlook of adulthood. The sonnet, "A Jesu-Cristo" and the poems "Señor" and "Nocturno" from *Cerebro y Corazón* (1922) represent the voice of an apparent believer imbued with child-like faith;[22] but it is a short-lived faith, for "Salmo lírico" begins to show disillusionment and a loss of faith. Judas comes alive and Christ dies; Evil prevails over Good, and Falsehood over Truth; Satan, Vice and Gold are worshipped; the "Lily of hope" vanishes and materialism triumphs. As his vision of the world changes so does his vague faith in Christianity.[23] "Canción filial" begins to show signs of rebellion by 1929 when he declares that he is willing to pray only to his own dead father, and then proceeds to direct a special prayer in sonnet form.[24]

In "Elegía" this stance hardens into a critical look at the role of the Church in Caribbean history. The early missionaries and conquistadors are not seen as envoys of the Holy Spirit but as pirates and messengers of an "Evil Spirit" and agents of the evils of colonialism.[25] "Elegía a un soldado vivo" stresses the role of the Church in pacifying the masses and crushing outbursts of resistance through the image of the "machete crucified on a cross".[26]

In "Mi patria es dulce por fuera..." God is painted in colours of hardened indifference towards the anguish of suffering humanity. The ending of the poem implies that man has to snatch his destiny out of the hands of God and take full control of his own circumstances by fighting the forces of oppression.[27]

"Elegía a Jesús Menéndez" goes one step further to ridicule the Christian faith and its rituals or prayer and worship and turns towards the Revolutionary faith inspired by the messianic Trade Union warrior, Jesús Menéndez. In "El cosmonauta" the rejection of God and religious faith is complete, and to make the rejection effective, the poet uses the very terminology and symbolism of the Christian faith - the rending of the veil and the evacuation of the divine throne.[28]

WOMEN, SEX AND LOVE:

Women. sensuality and love are three related subjects in which an intimate, personal interest can be identified in Guillén's poetry. Women are presented in various roles and guises that embrace both the erotic and the platonic, the crudely realistic and the idyllic, the carnal and the spiritual. The vision of the poet may be tinged with touches of lechery and romanticism, or disappointment and joy, but it is all expressed with a sense of honesty, and openness that is aptly summarised in "Digo que no soy un hombre puro" where he mocks the "purists" and the hypocritical "saints" and "angels":

> I am not telling you that I am a pure man,
> I am not saying that, but the contrary.
> I love (women, naturally),
> for my love can tell its name),
> and I like to eat pork with chips,
> and chickpeas and sausages, and
> eggs, chicken, mutton, duck,
> fish and seafood,
> and I drink rum and beer and brandy and wine,
> and I fornicate...
> Completely impure
> Nevertheless
> I believe there are many pure things in the world
> which are nothing more than pure feces.[29]

Woman, in Guillén's poetry is a human figure with multiple faces. At one level she is presented in the stereotyped role accorded to Negro and mulatto women by the white practitioners of the *Negrista* movement of the twenties and thirties: Guillén occasionally appears to allow himself to be trapped in that lascivious self-indulgence of seeing the black woman as a sex symbol whose overpowering sexual appeal has to be captured in the imagery of animals and grinding sugar mills. His Negress in "Mujer nueva" emerges like a somewhat primitive creature who brings to the unpublished word, a strong rump (*anca*), voice, teeth and tireless dancing feet.[30] Then in "Rumba" she is depicted in the following terms:

Spice of the hip,
Flexible, gilt croup (*grupa*)...

In the water of your wrapper
sail all my desires...
What desire to get shipwrecked
in that warm, deep sea:[31]

The "Madrigal" of *West Indies Ltd.* expands on this note of sensuality, seeing her as a "challenger of genital rage (whose) gait manufactures equine foam between (her) metal thighs for (her) screaming spasm".[32] But one need not be taken in by what seems either to be the lecherous eye of the poet[33] or a superficial "white" view of the black woman.

While still concentrating on such external and sensuous factors as the colour of the skin, the odour of sweat, the natural rhythmic movements of walking and dancing and the obvious sexual attraction of the black woman, Guillén appreciates her at another level and sees those very external factors as being part of a rich complex of potentialities and meanings. The mulatto woman in "Secuestro de la mujer de Antonio" whose "rumps will grind the sugar harvest of (her) sweat" possesses qualities which are not just sexual, but cultural and spiritual. She is *both* the "mulatto woman of fine gold" who can face up to hungry, male desire in "El negro mar" or who fires the imagination and lust of the male onlooker in "Agua del recuerdo",[34] and the black woman of the second "madrigal" in *Sóngoro Cosongo* whose "belly knows more than (her) head and as much as (her) thighs".[35] This immediately takes us beyond the mere delights and excitement of sensuality. It does not seem to be just another negative and stereo-typed description of the black woman whose only attributes are to be found in her agility as a dancer and in her sexual prowess. Rather, it seems to imply a rejection of that false bind that always elevates western rationalism and intellectualism to a position of primacy, and a revelation of the centrality of the belly and the pelvis to the sensibility, strength and creativity of the Negro, and to the powerful, spontaneous, emotional and spiritual forces that can be generated through that central source of energy and vitality.[36]

The emphasis on physical appearance, apart from its psycho-cultural meanings for the Negro who rejects Graeco-Latin concepts of beauty and recognises a valid Negroide basis for beauty and worth, draws attention to the folly of female vanity: the mulatto woman in "Mulata" (*Sóngoro Cosongo*) and the caucasion-like woman of "El abuelo" are both upbraided for their false notions of superiority. It also points towards the poet's own personal appreciation for the combination of physical strength and beauty and moral and spiritual resourcefulness in women. His prose-poem, "Nancy", dedicated to the Cuban poetess, Nancy Morejón, pays tribute to feminine charm, naturalness, and strength of character:

> "I like her smile, her dark flesh, her African head,
> her unroasted head, mentioned in reference to those
> roasters and roasted bourgeois Negroes who burn their
> hair every week and live as slaves to the deceptive
> hair-dresser"[37]

The physical interest serves as the entrée to those deeper perceptions hinted at in "A Julieta":

> And, yet, Julieta
> I try to know more.
> There is eating me out a secret
> desire to find out what there is behind
> that you, like a lightning flash that cuts across
> a slice of sky;
> ...I want to climb to the highest point
> of your spirit...[38]

That search for a relationship on an elevated plane where one derives a personal sense of fulfilment, is a constant feature of Guillén's love poems. In the very early phase of his writing, this search assumed definite romantic, pastoral and idyllic proportions in poems such as "Mariposa", "La balada azul" and "Madrigal" (from *Cerebro y Corazón*), and showed later resonances in poems like "Nocturno" (from *Poemas de amor*), or "A veces" (from *La rueda dentada*). As a kind of second phase development, the search took on the form of the Modernist pursuit of the aristocratic and perhaps even the platonic, in poems such as "Mariposa de cristal", "Madrigal trirrimo" or "Poema de las manos amables" (from *Cerebro y corazón*). From the tears, laments, sighs, whispers and joys of the pastoral tradition. shared in gardens, meadows, streams and on sea-shore, he moves to the adornment, estacy, and celestial experiences of palaces. In due course, these are rejected as inadequate pathways to fulfilment for the poet:

> A poet without false grief
> nor the yearning for death,
> but with the simple joy of going
> after you ... running after you ...[39].

One alternative is possession, perhaps even just partial physical possession as in "Un poem de amor":

> A mere touch, an electric contact,
> a surreptitious hug, a glance,
> a heart throb
> shouting, howling with a silent voice.[40]

Or it may be the most intense form of sexual possession as in "Piedra de horno" where:

> A river of promises descends from your hair,
> pauses in your breasts,
> and jellies finally in a puddle of molasses in
> your belly,
> rapes your firm flesh of nocturnal secret.
> Burning coal and baking stone...[41.]

Or it might yet even be an idealistic and spiritual possession like that he shares with his wife Rosa Portillo in the poem "Rosa tú, melancólica":

> My soul flies
> looking for you in the distance...
>
> from my narrow sheet
> I touch your firm body
>
> And in the night loaded
> with burning silence,
> Rosa, melancholy
> rose of my recollection,
> golden, living and moist,
> you descend from the roof,
> take my cold hand
> and stand by looking at me...
>
> a long fixed stare
> like a dream dagger.[42.]

But even possession in all its forms seems inadequate for providing that elusive fulfilment, for one can never be sure of the permanence and security of possession. "Tercera canción" states this dilemma in paradoxical terms:

> When I did not have you, I had you;
> when I wanted to have you, I lost you.[43]

"Soneto" from the same collection presents it in anguished, lyrical notes of uncertainty:

> Near you, why see you so far away?
> why say night if it is midday...
>
> Ay, why this having you without having you?[44.]

"Jugabas con un lápiz ..." (from *Poemas de amor*) and "Glosa #3" (from *El son entero*) deal with the problem in terms of an interplay of distance and proximity and the ironic coupling of physical presence and spiritual isolation, whereas "La muerte es un suplicio" and "Vino ud. de tan lejos" go further to describe any such pursuit of possession as groping in the dark for the incorporeal.

The real problem seems to be the complexity of the ideal being pursued. The poet wavers between notions of love and friendship in a poem like "Si a mi me hubieran dicho", or in "A Julieta" where he claims:

> "I look for you. You obsess me, although in truth
> at this height I don't know wheterr it is love
> or friendship."[45.]

But then for him, woman can be a real enigma, as in "Teresa" (from *Poemas de amor*) or "Rima ingenua" (from *Cerebro y corazón*).

The only answer seems to rest in a realistic acceptance of the joys and sorrows, strengths and weaknesses of woman in her real human context. The Poet's early definition of the composite woman with all the crudities, charms and contradictions of reality in "Mujer" seems to stand unchallenged:

> Woman: absolute synthesis
> of all that is good and great
> and bad and small.
> Harmonious combination of good and evil.

Union of the infinite
and the finite ...
Pain is your redemption ...
The pain of losing your virginity
and the pain of motherhood.[46]

She is the all-embracing symbol who represents: the concerns of motherhood in "Balada del güije" (from West Indies Ltd.) or "Doña María" (from *La paloma de vuelo popular*), or even "Manos, las de la Madre" (from "Poema de las manos amables" in *Cerebro y corazón*); the image of the "bad woman" who in *Motivos de son* is prostitute, deserting lover, and desperate and nagging concubine; the unfaithful woman of "Chéverre" (from *Songoro Cosongo*) who provokes her man to commit murder; or the inescapable cause of man's anxieties, disquietudes, disappointments, frustrations and lyrical outbursts as in "La vida empieza a correr...", "La vida pidiendo amor", "Agua del recuerdo", "Pero que te pueda ver", "El negro mar" and "Glosa" (from *El son entero*).

This personal element in the overall work of Guillén helps to delineate the scope for dealing with individual concerns even within the Revolutionary process. The question of individual integrity and anguish, or individual challenge, encounter and action as an essential part of the collective experience and collective awareness is answered by his refusal to smother the utterances of that personal Muse.

NOTES

1. Guillén, *Obra poética*, Vol. 1, pp. 86-87.
2. Ibid. p. 93.
3. Ibid. pp. 151-152.
4. Ibid. p. 135.
5. Guillén, *Obra poética*, Vol. II, p.8.
6. Guillén, *Obra poética*, Vol. I., p. 22.
7. Guillén, *Obra poética*, Vol. II, p. 321.
8. Ibid. p. 299.
9. I. Corinthians 15: 54-55.
10. Guillén, *Obra poética*, Vol. I. pp. 96-98.
11. Ibid. p. 399.
12. Guillén, *Obra poética*, Vol. I, p. 416.
13. Ibid. p. 394.
14. Guillén, *Obra poética*, Vol. II, p. 354.
15. Ibid. pp. 346-348.
16. Ibid. p. 350.
17. Guillén, *Obra poética* Vol. II, p. 409.
18. Ibid. p. 436.
19. Guillén, *Obra poética* Vol. II, p. 353.
20. Guillén, *Obra poética* Vol. I, p. 192.

21. Ibid. p. 98.

22. Ibid. 11, 15, 41.

23. Ibid. pp. 47-48.

24. Ibid. pp. 97-98.

25. Ibid. pp. 239-240.

26. Ibid. p. 189.

27. Ibid. pp. 225-227.

28. Guillén, *Obra poética*, Vol. II, pp. 282-283.

29. Ibid. p. 297.

30. Guillén, *Obra poética*, Vol. I, pp. 120-121.

31. Ibid. p. 123.

32. Ibid. p. 140.

33. For other poems dealing with sex, see *Obra poética*, Vol. II: "Piedra de horno" (pp. 212-213); "Señora" (p. 230); "Papaya" (p. 241); "El chulo" (p. 244).

34. Ibid, p. 252 and 249.

35. Ibid. p. 181.

36. See Edward Brathwaite's comment on the concept of the belly as the focus of an alternative tradition in *BIM* No. 45, July-Dec. 1967, pp. 39-40.

37. Guillén's *Obra Poética* Vol. II. p. 335.

38. Ibid. pp. 203-204

39. Ibid. p. 201.

40. Ibid. p. 208.

41. Ibid. p. 213.

42. Guillén, *Obra Poetica*, Vol. I. pp. 258-259.

43 Guillén's *Obra poética* Vol. II, p. 220.

46. Ibid. p. 218.

45. Ibid. p. 202.

46 Guillén's *Obra poética*, Vol. I., pp. 30-31.

CONCLUSION

The full poetic trajectory of Guillén is one that ranges from the position of "El mal del siglo" of 1922 to that of the historical overview of *El diario que a diario* (1972). The early stance of 1922 is that of the Modernist escapist who shuns the envy, calumny, egoism, greed, treachery and cowardice that characterise his age and opts for the "ivory tower" withdrawal from turpitude and mundane preoccupations of his environment:

> I cannot live in this age
> bereft of brain and soul.
> My lord: I am eagle or swan:
> Give me some lofty peak, like the eagle
> where I can empty
> my lyrical nostalgia,
> or like the swan, give me
> as some supreme grace,
> a silent and solitary lake
> with blue waves and white foam...[1]

But by 1927, this youthful Darío-like enthusiasm for the purity and serenity of the "ivory tower" gives way to the more militant passion for involvement and struggle that leads to the Revolutionary commitment of the later years.

During this period, two major factors that have contributed to the enduring quality of his *Obra poética* are: the combination of stylistic simplicity and accesssibility with formal variety - *romance, décima, letrilla, silva, canción, redondilla, son,* ballad, sonnet, elegy, madrigal, riddles; and the diversity of his satirical modes and thematic interests. His inventiveness and skill in the use of poetic forms have not excluded the people from the ambit of his readership. His is an art form placed squarely at the service of the people without scarificing thematic variety or artistic quality of recognizable worth.

If the criteria for the people's continued acceptance of, and faith in, his work as a classic have anything to do with the local relevance or the universality of his message, his depth of understanding of the intimate throbbings of the people's pulse, their aspirations and their vision of themselves, or his mastery of traditional and popular poetic forms, then Guillén has undoubtedly established his place in Cuba alongside Cervantes and Shakespeare in their respective national contexts, as interpreters of the soul of their people.

NOTES

1. Guillén, *Obra poética*, Vol. I., pp. 19-20.

SELECTED BIBLIOGRAPHY

1. WORKS BY NICOLÁS GUILLÉN

A. POETRY

Motivos de son. La Habana, Rambla, Bouza y Cía., 1930. 12 p., 14 cm.

Sóngoro Cosongo: Poemas mulatos. La Habana, Ucar, García y Cía., 1931. 56 p., 20 cm.

West Indies Ltd. Poemas. La Habana, Ucar, García y Cía., 1934. 48 p., 22 cm.

Cantos para soldados y sones para turistas. Prólogo de Juan Marinello, Grabados de José Chávez Morado. México, Masas, 1937. 87 p., ilus., 24 cm.

España. Poema en curato angustias y una esperanza. Mexico, Ed. México Nuevo, 1937. 22 p., 31 cm.

El son entero. Suma poética. 1929-1946. Con una carta de Muguel de Unamuno. Texos musicales de Eliseo y Emilo Grenet, Alejandro García Caturla y Silvestre Revueltas. Illustraciones de Carlos Enríquez. Buenos Aires, Ed. Pleamar, 1947. 210 p., ilus., música, 22 cm. (Coleccción Mirto).

La paloma de vuelo popular. Elegías. Buenos Aires, Ed. Losada, 1958. 157 p., 19 cm. (Bib. Contemporánea, s/n.) 2 da. ed. 1965.

Tengo. Prólogo de José Antonio Portundo. La Habana, Ed. del Consejo Nacional de Universidades, Universidad Central de las Villas, 1964. 197

p., 20 cm. (Caricatura por Juan David. Textos musicales de Ignacio Villa "Bola de Nieve", J. González Allué y Juan Blanco).

Poemas de amor. La Habana, Ed. La Tertulia, 1964. 57 p., 19 cm. (cuadernos de Poesía, 6).

Antología mayor. La Habana, Bolsilibros Unión, 1964. 292 p., 16 cm.

El gran Zoo. La Habana, Ed. Unión. Ilus. Fayad Jamís; cubierta, E. Abela Alonso. 88 p., 21 cm. (Col. Contemporáneos).

La rueda dentada. La Habana, Ed. UNEAC, 1972, 131 p. (Contemporáneos)

El diario que a diario. La Habana, Ed. UNEAC, 1972, 87 p. (Cuadernos Girón).

Obra poética: 1920-1958 (Tomo I). Instituto Cubano de libro, La Habana, 1972, ed Angel Augier, 570 p.

Obra poética: 1958-1972 (Tomo II). (1973). ed. Anguel Augier. 572 p.

B. PROSE

Prosa de prisa (crónicas) Iniversidad Central de Las Villas, 1962, ed. Angel Augier. 343 p.

Prosa de prisa: 1929-1972 (Tomo I), Editorial Arte y Literatura, La Habana, 1975 ed. Angel Augier. 423 p.

Porsa de prisa: 1929-1972 (Tomo II), 1976, Augier. 452 p.

Cronista en tres épocas, Editora Política, La Habana 1984, 199 p.

C. TRANSLATIONS INTO ENGLISH

Cuba libre. Los Angeles, Cal., Anderson and Ritchie, The Ward Ritchie Press, 1948. 98 p., ilus, 28 cm. Trad. por Langston Hughes y Ben F. Carruthers. Ilus por Gar Gilbert.

!Patria o muerte! The great Zoo and other poems. Edited and translated by Robert Márquez. 223 p. Dibujo de Martin Slephen Moskof. New York, Monthly Review Press, 1972.

Man Making Words. Selected poems... translated, annotated with an introduction by Robert Márquez and David Arthur McMurray. University of Massachusetts Press, 1972. 214 p.

2. CRITICISM

A. BOOKS

Augier, Angel. *Nicolás Guillén. Notas para estudio biográfico crítico.* (T.I.), La Habana, Direc. de Publicaciones de Universidad Central de Las Villas, 1962. 237 p; 2 da. ed., 1965, 308 p.; (T. II) 1964, 299 p. (Reeditados en Nicolás Guillén La Habana, Col. Contemporáneos, UNEAC, 1971, 318 p.)

Coulthard, G.R. *Race and Colour in Caribbean Literature* (Oxford University Press, 1962.) 118 p.

Coulthard, G.R. *Raza y color en la literatura antillana.* Sevilla, Col. Mar Adentro, 1958.

Dawes, Neville *Prolegomena to Caribbean Literature* Kingston, Institute of Jamaica, 1977.

Gaetani, Francis Marion. *Nicolás Guillén: A Study on the Fonology and Metrics in his Poetry.* M.A. Essay, New York, Columbia University, 1940.

Janneinz, Juan. *A Bibliography of Neo-African Literature: from Africa, America and the Caribbean,* London, André Deutsch, 1965. XXXV 359 p.

Martínez Estrada, Ezequiel. *La poesia afrocubana de Nicolás Guillén.* Motevideo, Ed. Arca, 1966. (Ensayo y testimonio, 4). 92 p., 2 da. ed., La Habana, Cuadernos Union, 1967. 93 p.

Morejón, Nancy. *Recopilacíon de textos sobre Nicolás Guillén* (CASA de las Américas, La Habana, 1972.), 374 p.

Morejón, Nancy, *Nación y mestizaje en Nicolás Guillén,* La Habana, Ediciones Union, 1982.

Sardinha, Dennis. *The Poetry of Nicolás Guillén - An Introduction,* London, 1976, 80 p.

B. ARTICLES

Allen, Martha E. "Nicolás Guillén, poeta del pueblo" *Rivista Iberoamericana.* México, febrero-julio, 1949.

Augier, Angel. "Raíz cubana de Nicolás Guillén." *La Ultima Hora,* a. II no. 23, p. 6, 36-37, 10 julio de 1952.

"Poesía de Cuba en Nicolás Guillén: Su expresión plástica," *Union,* La Habana, a I, No. 2, p. 61-78, julio - agusto, 1962.

Augier, Angel. "Alusiones africanas en la poesía se Nicolás Guillén". *Santiago*, revista de la Universidad de Oriente, Santiago de Cuba, no. 5, diciembre de 1971, p. 177-223.

Coulthard, G.R. "The emergence of Afro-cuban poetry". *Caribbean Quarterly*, v. II, no. 4, p. 15. 1954.

Coulthard, G.R. "Nicolás Guillén and West Indian Negritude". *Caribbean Quartely*, v. 16, no. I, p. 52, March, 1970.

Depestre, René. "Nicolás Guillén: Orfeo negro de Cuba", *La Gaceta de Cuba*, La Habana, no. 4, 1969.

Ellis, Kieth. "Literary Americanism and the Recent Poetry of Nicolás Guillén". *University of Toronto Quarterly*, (UTQ), Vol. XLV, No. I. Fall, 1975, pp. 1-18.

Ellis, Keith. "Nicolás Guillén and Derek Walcott: Reflections on a Study by Neville Dawes", *Caribbean Literature in Comparison*, Kingston, 1990, p. 45-55, ed. J.R. Pereira.

Fernandez Retamar, R. "Nicolás Guillén" en *La poesía contemporánea de Cuba* (1927-1953). La Habana, *Orígenes* 1954. (Poesía negra", p. 45-62; "Poesía social", p. 63-75)

Ferrand, Manuel. "Raíz española en la poesía de Nicolás Guillén". Estudios Americanos. Sevilla nov.-dic., 1954.

Irish, J.A.G. "Notes on a Historic Visit", *Caribbean Quarterly*, Vol. 21, No. I, 1975, p. 74-84.

King, Lloyd. "Mr. Black in Cuba", *African Studies Association of the West Indies.* (ASAWI) Bulletin, No. 5, Dec. 1972, pp. 21-26.

King, Lloyd. "Nicolás Guillén and Afrocubanismo", *A Celebration of Black and African Writing*, ed. Bruce King and Kolawole Ogungberan, Ahmadu Bello University Press and Oxford University Press Nigeria, 1975, pp. 30-45.

Lewis, Rupert. "Nicolás Guillén - Poet-laureate of the Cuban Revolution'. *Daily News*. Dec. I, 1974.

Marinello, Juan. "Poesía negra. Apuntes desde Guillén y Ballagas", en *Poética. Ensavos en Entusiasmo*. Madrid, Espasa Calpe, 1933, p.101-103.

Melon, Alfred. "Guillén, poeta de las síntesis", *Union*, La Habana, a. 14, no. 4, p. 96-132, dic. 1970.

Portuondo, José A. "En busca del entero". *Hoy*, La Habana, 6-7-, mayo 1943, p. 4.

ABOUT THE AUTHOR

J.A. George Irish

J.A. George Irish is currently the Director of the Caribbean Research Center at Medgar Evers College of The City University of New York. He is also Professor of Caribbean and Latin American Studies in the Department of Interdisciplinary Studies in the same institution.

He has a special interest in the literature of Latin America and the Caribbean, and particularly the literary treatment of the African experience across the Americas.

Dr. Irish was Head of the Department of Spanish at the University of the West Indies when Nicolás Guillén was invited to visit that University on two occasions in his capacity as one of the Caribbean's most distinguished literary figures. On the first occasion, he gave a series of public lectures and readings of his poetry, and the second occasion was for the award of the Honorary Degree of Doctor of Letters.

Dr. Irish has personally designed and taught courses on Spanish Caribbean and Latin American literature, and has supervised numerous theses and dissertations in the same area.

ISBN 976-8039-05-1